# Parenting Children with ADHD + Workbook 2-in-1

Simple Strategies to Manage Explosive Behavior & Random Meltdowns, Exercises to Improve Communication, Mindfulness and More Through Peaceful Methods

**Natalie Morgan**

Copyright © 2024 by Natalie Morgan

All rights reserved.

No portion of this book may be reproduced in any form without written permission from the publisher or author, except as permitted by U.S. copyright law.

# Table of Contents

## Parenting Kids with ADHD

**Introduction** .................................................................................................................. 12

### Chapter 1: Mindfully Managing Your Child's ADHD ............................................... 15
- What Is ADHD? ............................................................................................................ 15
- Can We Rule it Out? .................................................................................................... 16
- The Benefits of Evaluation .......................................................................................... 17
- EXERCISE: Emphasize the Positive! ............................................................................ 17
- EXERCISE: Evaluating the Impact of Your Child's ADHD ........................................... 18
- What is Mindfulness? .................................................................................................. 19
- EXERCISE: Mindful Eating ........................................................................................... 20
- Mindful Parenting and ADHD: Beginning the Journey ............................................... 21
- Action Plan: Mindfully Managing ADHD in Children .................................................. 22

### Chapter 2: ADHD and Executive Function ............................................................... 24
- Executive Function and ADHD .................................................................................... 24
- ADHD and Brain Management Control ....................................................................... 25
- EXERCISES: Reframing the Parental View of Executive Function ............................. 26
- The Challenge of Task Completion ............................................................................. 28
- Mindfulness and Stress ............................................................................................... 28
- EXERCISE: Using S.T.O.P. ............................................................................................ 29
- EXERCISE: Awareness of Breath ................................................................................. 29
- Informal Mindfulness ................................................................................................... 29
- EXERCISE: Daily Informal Mindfulness ....................................................................... 30
- Action Plan: Bringing Awareness to Your Child's ADHD ............................................ 30

### Chapter 3: Why Your Self-Care is Important to Your Child .................................. 32
- The Impact of ADHD On Parents ................................................................................. 32
- EXERCISE: Give Yourself a Break ............................................................................... 33
- Taking Baby Steps Toward Change ............................................................................ 33
- EXERCISE: Decluttering ............................................................................................... 34
- Attention Matters: Do You Also Have ADHD? ............................................................ 35
- EXERCISE: Compile a Behavioral Triage List ............................................................. 36
- Self-Care Can Help You Get Unstuck From Stress ..................................................... 36
- EXERCISE: Paying Attention to Your Stress ............................................................... 37

Make Time For Self-Care................................................................................................................37
EXERCISE: Focus On the Joy in Life .........................................................................................38
Action Plan: Caring for the Caregiver ....................................................................................38

## Chapter 4: Change Begins With You..........................................................................................39
Reframing Difficult Experiences ..............................................................................................39
The Dangers of Compounding Difficult Experiences.........................................................40
EXERCISE: Separating Experiences........................................................................................40
Seizing the Reins.........................................................................................................................40
EXERCISE: Fifteen Breaths.........................................................................................................41
Fostering Independence and The Executive Function Toolkit.........................................41
Perfection is a Thief of Happiness...........................................................................................42
EXERCISE: Watch the Weather ................................................................................................44
The Rippling Effect of ADHD ....................................................................................................44
EXERCISE: Reframe the Parental View On Academic Challenges ................................45
Action Plan: Externalize.............................................................................................................45

## Chapter 5: Communication and Mindfulness for ADHD................................................47
How ADHD Impacts Communication....................................................................................47
Finding the Middle Ground .....................................................................................................48
EXERCISE: Tally Talking Time ..................................................................................................48
Actions vs Words: Helping Your Child Repair Communication Flaws ..........................48
EXERCISE: Celebrate Communication Success..................................................................49
Mindfulness and Communication..........................................................................................50
EXERCISE: Imagine Communicating Advice to Friends...................................................50
EXERCISE: What's Your Communication Style?..................................................................51
Action Plan: Practice Mindful Communication ..................................................................52

## Chapter 6: Using Targeted Praise and Rewards for Success .........................................53
Behavioral Training & Reward Systems ................................................................................53
EXERCISE: Keep a Gratitude Journal.....................................................................................54
EXERCISE: Establishing a Reward System ...........................................................................54
Using Mindfulness in Praise & Rewards ................................................................................55
Cut Yourself Some Slack ............................................................................................................56
EXERCISE: Give Yourself a Much-Needed Break................................................................56
Action Plan: Focus on Positives in Behavioural Planning.................................................57

## Chapter 7: How to Handle Difficult Behaviors ...................................................................58
Building a Foundation and Creating Boundaries...............................................................58
How to Modify Behavior: Time-Outs .....................................................................................60

Grocery Store Meltdowns: What To Do ........................................................................................ 60
EXERCISE: Ground Yourself ........................................................................................................... 61
EXERCISE: Mindfully Setting Boundaries ..................................................................................... 63
The Wings That Make Mindfulness .............................................................................................. 63
Action Plan: Ways To Address a Future Behavioral Crisis ......................................................... 64

## Chapter 8: Education and ADHD .................................................................................. 65
Executive Function, School Performance, and Policy ................................................................ 65
Create an Educational Plan and Influence the System .............................................................. 66
Keep Mindfulness in Mind .............................................................................................................. 66
EXERCISE: Mindfully Moving .......................................................................................................... 67
Action Plan: Assist With Your Child's Academic Success .......................................................... 68

## Chapter 9: ADHD Medication Options ........................................................................ 69
Medication Facts and Myths .......................................................................................................... 69
Pros and Cons of Medication ........................................................................................................ 70
EXERCISE: Mindfully Making Decisions ....................................................................................... 71
EXERCISE: Employing Loving-Kindness ...................................................................................... 72
Action Plan: Make Treatment Decisions that Benefit Your Child ............................................. 72

## Conclusion ............................................................................................................................ 74

## References ........................................................................................................................... 76

# ADHD Workbook for Kids (5-11)

## Introduction ......................................................................................................................... 84
Welcome to my ADHD Workbook For Kids. ................................................................................ 84
What is ADHD? ................................................................................................................................. 85
What is Executive Function? .......................................................................................................... 86
How to Use this Workbook ............................................................................................................ 87

## Hello from the World of ADHD ..................................................................................... 88
Hello parents, ................................................................................................................................... 88
Hello kids, .......................................................................................................................................... 89

## Chapter 1: ADHD & Me ..................................................................................................... 90
What is ADHD? ................................................................................................................................. 91
1. Mix & Match Activity .................................................................................................................... 92
2. The Truth About ADHD ............................................................................................................... 93

3. What Are ADHD Symptoms, and What Symptoms Do I Have? ......97
  4. The Sunny Side of ADHD ......100
  5. ADHD Success Stories ......101

## Chapter 2: I Am Stronger than ADHD ...... 103
  6. What Does ADHD Look Like? ......103
  7. What Do YOU Look Like? ......104
  8. What Do YOU Look Like with ADHD? ......104
  9. Your Vision Collage ......105
  10. What Does Organization Look Like to You? ......107
  12. You Are Stronger than ADHD ......111
  13. It's Time for Big Feelings ......112
  14. Distractions, Distractions, Everywhere! ......118
  15. Treasure Trove ......120

## Chapter 3: How to Make Good Choices ...... 121
  16. Stop. Think! ......121
  17. What Did You Say? ......125
  18. Pick the Right Choice ......126
  19. Red Light, Green Light! ......129
  20. Bake a Cake ......130
  21. Repeat the Beat! ......131
  22. Tell Me What You Are Doing ......132
  23. Simon Says ......132
  24. Questions & Answers ......133
  25. The Tower Game ......134
  26. Would You Rather? ......134

## Chapter 4: Healthy Body, Healthy Mind ...... 136
  Your Brain on Food ......136
  The Positive and Negative Effects of Food ......137
  The Best Way to Eat ......137
  27. Coloring My Body with Healthy Food ......138
  28. Brain Food ......138
  29. What Can I Do? ......140
  30. I'm Booooored. Now What? ......141
  31. Reading for Fun? ......142
  32. Questions and Answers ......143
  33. Guess the Good Food ......144
  34. Mindfulness & Meditation ......145

 35. You Want me to do Yoga? ............................................................. 148
 36. Music & Me .................................................................................. 150

**Chapter 5: ADHD at Home** ............................................................... **151**
 37. Pretend & Play ............................................................................ 151
 38. Helping at Home ........................................................................ 152
 39. See It. Say It. .............................................................................. 152
 40. Memory ...................................................................................... 153
 41. Have Fun with It! ....................................................................... 153
 42. Find an Item, Put It Away! ......................................................... 154
 43. Decorate Your Workspace ......................................................... 154
 44. Sing-a-Long ................................................................................ 154
 45. How About a Board Game? ....................................................... 154

**Chapter 6: ADHD at School** ............................................................... **156**
 46. First Thing in the Morning ........................................................ 156
 47. Lunch & Recess .......................................................................... 157
 48. Coming Home ............................................................................ 158
 49. Chair or No Chair ....................................................................... 159
 50. Desk Cleanliness ........................................................................ 159
 51. Fun Pens, Pencils, Notebooks, and More! ................................ 159
 52. Positive Feedback, Positive Results .......................................... 160
 53. Fidget Tools, Anyone? ............................................................... 160

**Chapter 7: Friends & Family** ............................................................. **161**
 54. Time to Take Turns .................................................................... 161
 55. Practice Kindness with Words ................................................... 162
 56. Share & Share Alike ................................................................... 162
 57. Helping Hand at Home .............................................................. 163
 58. Helping Hand at School ............................................................. 164
 59. Writing Letters to Friends ......................................................... 164
 60. Structured Play with Friends .................................................... 165

**Chapter 8: Getting Ready** ................................................................. **166**
 61. Prep List for Tomorrow ............................................................. 166
 62. Good Days. Bad Days. ................................................................ 166
 63. Clothing, Pajamas, Drawers, & Closets ..................................... 167
 64. Shoes & School Tools ................................................................. 168
 65. Rooms & Work Areas ................................................................. 168

## Chapter 9: I Am Ready! .......................................................................................... 170
    66. A Gold Star for Good Behavior ........................................................... 170
    67. Build Your Own Checklist .................................................................. 170
    68. Reflecting on You ............................................................................. 171
    69. What Else Are You Missing? ............................................................. 171
    70. You're Ready! ................................................................................... 172

## References ............................................................................................................ 173

## Resources for Grown-ups ................................................................................ 174

## Resources for Kids ........................................................................................... 175

# Parenting Kids with ADHD

Managing Your Child's Explosive Behavior Through Peaceful Methods, Improving Emotional Control & Self-Regulation To Nurture Their Developing Mind to Live a Fulfilling Life!

**Natalie Morgan**

# Introduction

*"Why fit in when you were born to stand out?"*
- Dr. Seuss

Welcome to Parenting Kids With ADHD In order to maximize the benefits of this book it is recommended to acquire the Workbook in this series.

In a society where differences are seen as a bad thing, everyday life can be difficult for children with Attention Deficit Hyperactivity Disorder (ADHD) and the parents raising them. When parenting children with ADHD, there are certain struggles that neurologically typical children may never have to deal with. These struggles can include epic meltdowns, unnecessary arguing, and the appearance of not listening. All of these struggles can make a parent feel like they're running in circles and making no progress.

Many times, parents may feel like they're losing their mind trying to make their young child with ADHD listen to them without fully understanding that the child may simply not fully understand or comprehend what is being asked of them. Children with ADHD are known to be impulsive, struggle with their school work, and have difficulty settling down. As a result, many parents when under stress may resort to yelling, feeling like they're giving in too often for just a moment of peace and quiet, and have trouble staying calm in the face of their child's impulsive behavior. ADHD is known to increase familial stress, which will only make parenting a child with ADHD harder. This can create a cycle of anxiety and worry without peace and harmony in the family home. It's not just the family life that gets disrupted by ADHD, either. This attention disorder is the culprit for many social skill mishaps, communication mistakes, failure to follow through on morning and bedtime routines, poor eating habits, planning issues, and technology use or abuse. Many children with ADHD may have an especially difficult time when it's time to transition from one of the activities that they enjoy the most in order to do something they may not want to do as much, something that often causes outbursts and intense tantrums.

The presence of ADHD in a child can create patterns of unpredictability and unproductivity in caretakers and make parents feel weary and worn down quickly. This also creates another cycle, as this stress will inevitably impact the child and make them feel as if they are the culprit for all the stress and burden they are experiencing at home. No parent wants their child–especially one struggling with ADHD–to feel like a burden or stressor.

But there is hope. These maddening feelings and cycles are precisely why adopting mindfulness in parenting is essential to raising children with ADHD. In this book, you will not only learn what it means to have ADHD and how your child sees the world, but also how to speak to them on a level they will understand. All children are smart, but some need a little help understanding things their way. This may mean presenting instructions or giving commands in ways that are more beneficial, useful, and loving.

This book will assist you with the journey to understanding your child with ADHD and give you powerful parenting exercises that will have you and your child communicating in a healthier way, despite your child's age and your stress. The types of skills discussed in this book are that of practicing focus and attention, as well as personal awareness. Children with ADHD tend to operate on an auto-pilot mode, where they may not be entirely aware of themselves or the impact they have on a situation. By practicing awareness, children with ADHD and their parents can find solace and rationale in the consequences of actions.

This book is designed to assist with understanding mindfulness, its benefits, and its approach to ADHD symptoms. From there, we will discuss ADHD in length and detail, expanding on how ADHD interacts with the brain and how children with ADHD see the world around them. Each chapter will be filled with information and exercises on how to understand your child and how to quell the epic meltdowns that may occur from a child's impulsive nature. We will discuss self-care and why it is so important to parents raising a child with ADHD, so you'll know how you can properly care for yourself and show your child how to take care of themselves, as well.

Developing a new relationship with your situation, your child, and your mindful parenting style may be difficult, but the benefits are entirely worth the time and energy. By using all the exercises within this book and compatible workbook, you and your child will be able to communicate better and more clearly without all the yelling and flushed-face anger that only makes you more angry and your child more sad. As such, one of the biggest factors discussed in this book is proper discipline for a child with ADHD and how to handle the most challenging of behaviors.

Being mindful doesn't mean constant meditation. Mindfulness is more about fostering focus, flexibility, and peace for the whole family. Mindfulness means stopping during a stressful situation, accepting the present moment, and understanding how that moment is making you feel without feeling like you're about to lose your mind.

Parenting children is a difficult and rewarding journey, and raising children with ADHD can feel like a constant battle. The good news is that it does not have to feel that way. By employing all the methods and exercises included in this book to keep calm and open up an honest dialogue with your child, you and your family can break the cycles of stress, anxiety, and yelling.

Familial peace is at your fingertips. Continue reading to begin your journey to mindful parenting.

# Mindfully Managing Your Child's ADHD

Beginning the journey to manage your child's ADHD through mindful parenting can feel daunting at first, but the benefits of it can be incredible. First, however, we must look to understand the benefits of evaluating your child for ADHD and what ADHD really entails. From there, we will discuss mindfulness and how this approach to parenting can help you and your family deal with the struggles and challenges that may come with raising a child with ADHD. Throughout this chapter, there will be exercises to help you and your family incorporate this approach into daily life. These exercises will help you and your child focus on the positives of life instead of amplifying the negatives as well as evaluating how impactful the symptoms of ADHD are for the whole family.

## What Is ADHD?

ADHD is the acronym for Attention Deficit Hyperactivity Disorder, and it is one of the most common childhood disorders. This neurological disorder is reported by ADDitude magazine to affect between five and eleven percent of all American children (Williams). However prevalent, the symptoms can range from slight to severe. Many of the symptoms include a lack of attention, frequently forgetting what was just said, increased impulsivity, constant fidgeting, hyperactivity, frequent talking (more than a typical child), and trouble with patience. A big factor noticed by parents with their children who have ADHD is a difficulty in following instructions. Sometimes, children with ADHD–especially the younger children between three and five–can have epic meltdowns and tantrums that can leave parents feeling incredibly frustrated.

In order to understand whether or not your child truly has ADHD, we must first take a look at what ADHD is, what the symptoms look like in children, and what it means for your child to live with ADHD. Julie Rawe, from Understood.com, discusses how a child's brain with ADHD differs from that of a neurologically typical child: a large-scale MRI study funded by the National Institutes of Health "shows that some parts of the brain tend to be a little smaller and/or take longer to mature in kids with ADHD" (Rawe). Simply put, the brain in a child with ADHD needs a little longer to mature than that of a neurologically typical child. The brain's relationship to ADHD in children will be discussed in more detail in Chapter Two.

Keath Lowe from VeryWellMind.com discusses what ADHD is like for children: "Children may experience a broad spectrum of emotions, including frustration, feeling lost, disconnection, confusion, overwhelm, restlessness, [and] feeling out of control." Lowe continues by explaining that children with ADHD frequently get labeled as being bad, lazy, or dumb children, which could not be further from the truth.

## Can We Rule it Out?

Some children can be very active and hyper without having ADHD at all. In fact, "there is no single test to diagnose ADHD" (Diagnosing ADHD, n.d.). Instead, there is a comprehensive evaluation that children undergo to make a diagnosis and rule out other disorders. This evaluation is also important for determining co-existing conditions, such as Oppositional Defiance Disorder, for example. An evaluation of this caliber requires time and energy, as well as a detailed medical and family history. This kind of evaluation and diagnosis is made by psychologists, clinical social workers, neurologists, psychiatrists, pediatricians, and nurse practitioners.

The process of ruling out ADHD–or diagnosing a child with ADHD–is a rigorous one that includes biological and psychological considerations. In fact, many other mental health and neurological issues, like anxiety, depression, and some types of learning disabilities can often present with similar symptoms as ADHD. In special cases, such as Autsim Spectrum Disorder, another cause may be a primary diagnosis while comorbid with ADHD as a secondary diagnosis. During the evaluation, a thorough history will be examined from both parents and teachers of the child, as well as the child themselves, when necessary. The first step for diagnosing ADHD is to rule out any other underlying medical issues that could be causing the ADHD-like symptoms. Sometimes, these are the culprits and neurological intervention may not be necessary. In the cases that medical intervention and an evaluation are necessary, there are several mental health professionals that can help. The benefits of undergoing an evaluation cannot be overstated. In the next section, we will discuss these benefits.

## The Benefits of Evaluation

Children with ADHD often begin exhibiting symptoms as young as age four. It's about this time they get evaluated for ADHD, but most of the time, children are usually in kindergarten or first grade by the time they see a neurologist. Many times, parents will wait until the symptoms become disruptive to schooling and home life before they seek input from a medical professional. Every evaluation is different and every child is unique. Thus, a diagnosis for ADHD can mean different things for each child. For starters, it's important to remember that an accurate diagnosis is what guides families toward effective treatments. Without knowing what a child is dealing with, a parent may not be employing the best strategies and treatments. In fact, many people can be afflicted from deep sadness and depressive symptoms because their ADHD is not being taken care of in a way that addresses the root causes and they don't see any long-lasting solutions to their challenges.

By evaluating your child for ADHD, you and your child will have a headstart and a team of medical professionals who can decide whether or not medication, therapy, or other forms of treatment are necessary.

## EXERCISE: Emphasize the Positive!

Now that we know how important it is to have an evaluation for a child exhibiting symptoms of ADHD, it's time to focus on the positives. Having a child with any kind of disorder– even that of an attention disorder– can be overwhelming and scary. Many parents walk into the neurologists office scared out of their minds that their child will need medication that will take their personality away and leave them a shell of their former self. Most of the time, this simply doesn't happen. In fact, a study published in 2015 by the British Medical Journal, showed that the most common drug prescribed for ADHD improved symptoms and general behavior in children. The study showed that the drug's side-effects included only non-serious adverse effects which included a loss of appetite and trouble sleeping.

That being said, it's important to focus on all the positives in life and the situation as opposed to circling all the negatives associated with your child's diagnosis and future.

Instead of focusing on all the negatives, you may want to employ using positive affirmations to emphasize all the positives of your child's care and well-being. Here are several examples of positive affirmations to employ:

- My child is safe, healthy, and cared for.
- My child's ADHD is part of who they are.
- My child has access to great medical care.
- My child may not need medication.
- Our family may be able to rely on behavioral therapy to solve challenges.

By focusing only on the good things and not on the "what-if" scenarios involving your child's diagnosis, you and your family can rest a little easier and take each event and moment as it comes.

## EXERCISE: Evaluating the Impact of Your Child's ADHD

This exercise is all about setting aside some time and really thinking about your child's behavior and their ADHD. Since the evaluation and diagnosis parts are over, it's time to think about how your child's ADHD affects their life, your life, and your family. Sometimes, raising a child with ADHD can come with some extra struggles that can take a whole family by storm. What may have begun as normal child-like behavior may start to feel like it's out of control or happening too often. Children with ADHD often have trouble with the following symptoms:

- Easily distracted
- Not truly listening
- Difficulty paying attention
- Easily forgetting what was said
- Difficulty following instructions
- Requiring constant reminders
- Poor school performance
- Disorganized nature
- Constant climbing, jumping, or roughhousing during quiet playtime

- Constant fidgeting and inability to sit still
- Rushing through things and trouble with patience
- Making careless mistakes
- Constantly on-the-go
- Difficulty with controlling interruptions
- Blurting things out
- Not thinking about their actions, or the consequences of their actions
- Doing things they shouldn't, even when they know they shouldn't
- Trouble controlling emotions, losing their temper quickly, and lacking self-control or self-soothing abilities

Using the above list, take some time to write down all the ways your child's ADHD affects your family. Perhaps your child has trouble with emotional regulation and requires a lot of soothing that leaves you drained. Knowing that this is a consistent issue will aid you in figuring out how to help your child self-soothe and become more emotionally intelligent so that they can better control their emotions in the future. Try to think of all the effects you possibly can, as this can only arm you with more knowledge to help yourself and your child manage the impact of their ADHD in the home and in your relationship with your child.

Also remember that it's okay to feel frustrated and stressed. Many parents tend to first view their child's outbursts and symptoms as tantrums and misbehavior. While this can leave a lot of parents confused and feeling disrespected, there is hope for both yourself and your child. Learning about what root behaviors are the biggest issues that your child deals with most often can help alleviate some of the tension and anxiety in the home.

## What is Mindfulness?

The word mindfulness is tossed around a lot in the modern age of social media, but what does it really mean? In short, "mindfulness is the basic human ability to be fully present, aware of where we are and what we're doing, and not overly reactive or overwhelmed by what's going on around us" ("What Is Mindfulness?" n.d.). The idea behind mindfulness is to still the mind and be present in the current moment. While it's incredibly easy for the mind to wander and for you to be filled with anxiety and apprehension about the future, mindfulness attempts to keep you grounded in the current moment and remind you that there is little need to focus on anything else at that time.

When practicing mindfulness, it's entirely reasonable that your mind may drift off to worry about something, but by focusing on the current moment–on how your body feels seated, or how your legs are moving, or how your breathing is coming in and out–you can remain worry-free and focused on the present. The benefit of adopting mindfulness into your life is that it can help with being overly reactive about situations that stress you out. Instead of getting angry and stressed when the toilet gets clogged, mindfulness can help you accept the current moment and instead of getting overwhelmed, look for a solution (i.e. a plunger).

Some examples of mindfulness include: moving meditation which means paying careful attention to how your muscles, limbs, and body move while you walk, sit, or stand; short pauses in which you focus on breathing or an object; and combining meditation techniques like mindfulness alongside yoga or walking. In truth, mindfulness can be practiced anywhere.

Mindfulness is also known to reduce stress, improve work performance, help you gain awareness of yourself, and allow you to observe what happens in your mind as challenges come your way ("What is Mindfulness?" n.d.).

It's also important to note that mindfulness is not an obscure thing that requires extra purchases or overt change. It's simply the ability to think, "stop," and allow yourself to be present in the current moment. We know that "meditation begins and ends in the body. It involves taking the time to pay attention to where we are and what's going on, and that starts with being aware of our body…" ("What is Mindfulness?" n.d.). You may want to think of yourself floating in the clouds or the ocean and see how it calms your heart rate and removes you from external stressors.

Now that you know what mindfulness is and its purpose, you may now want to practice it in a real-life scenario. In the next section, you'll practice mindful eating, a technique that can help alleviate overeating and disordered eating.

## **EXERCISE: Mindful Eating**

Mindful eating is a great technique for those who are prone to eating too much, too fast. When we eat mindlessly, we tend to eat past the point at which we're full and may accidentally ignore some of the body's signals, eat to quell intense emotions and multitask while eating which will only make us unaware of when we're truly full. Instead, it's important to practice mindfulness while eating, even though some people may find it boring. To get started, you'll get your meal and find a quiet, distraction-free environment. Then, follow these steps:

1. Look at the plate of food in front of you, taking in how it looks, smells, and presents.

2. Take small bites, chewing slowly and not rushing the meal. Take time to savor the dish and truly understand the taste of each component in the dish.

3. Eat in silence, focusing only on the plate of food in front of you, on the way it may sound, look, and taste between bites.

4. Focus on the feelings you get both mentally and physically while eating. This is important to understand when you are done eating or if you need more food.

5. The moment at which you realize you are content, it's time to stop eating and set the food aside. Take a moment to note how much food is left on the plate and how much food you've eaten. This can be used as a guideline in the future to understand how much you truly need to feel satiated.

6. Ask yourself the purpose for which you are eating. Are you hungry? Are you bored? Are you eating simply because the food is tasty or healthy?

You can practice this exercise as often as desired, although one meal per day can suffice for many people beginning their mindfulness journey. By engaging in this mindfulness exercise, you can become more comfortable with the concept of being immersed in the moment and enjoying the present, as opposed to worrying over the past and future.

## Mindful Parenting and ADHD: Beginning the Journey

Although the journey may be challenging, being mindful in the face of your child's ADHD-related tantrums and unpleasantries can help you stay calm and react appropriately to impulsive and difficult behavior. Mindfulness is a practice that's been around for centuries, stemming from religions like Hinduism and Buddhism (Selva, 2021). From there, mindfulness was popularized in the East and West, becoming a tool that is often used to remain calm under the pressures of life.

In regards to managing ADHD in a child, mindfulness is used to refrain from screaming, yelling, or getting overly reactive with your child. Unfortunately, managing a child's ADHD meltdowns can cause an incredible amount of stress that can compound into very explosive reactions from parents. Instead, by pausing in the moment and taking a deep breath, you'll better understand and accept what is happening without resorting to screaming and losing your mind. Mindfulness means pausing to accept what is happening in the current moment and focusing on keeping yourself calm. Many times, parents are guided toward bringing attention to their breathing as a way to remain grounded. This means taking the present moment to focus only on breathing and trying to push out every other external factor from your mind. This can be done with nearly anything. While focusing on breathing is a good choice, some parents may want to focus on their bracelet and the colors of it. Some parents may prefer to focus on the feeling of their feet on the floor.

At this moment, so what if your child is throwing themselves on the floor? This moment is meant to help you, the parent, gather yourself and calm your own heart rate and stress levels down so that you can then help your child manage their ADHD symptoms without your own compounding stress. What this does is create a healthier and more resilient environment for the whole family.

This will take much time and practice, but with some work and effort, mindfulness can be achieved and implemented smoothly into your parenting plan.

## Action Plan: Mindfully Managing ADHD in Children

Now that you know all about ADHD and mindfulness, it's time to make a plan so as to implement your mindful parenting strategy into everyday life. You won't truly know what works until you've started implementing things, but having a rough draft action plan outlined will help you walk into tantrums a little easier.

Consider making a list of different things to bring your focus to during one of your child's meltdowns or tantrums. By having a few different options, you can experiment with them and figure out what works best for you. You may want to consider implementing two or three different methods in tandem, such as breathing while focusing on a poster.

From there, it's time to put it into action. When a meltdown or tantrum comes your way, use the mindfulness technique to bring your focus to the present moment and try to ground yourself to peace and calmness.When you feel ready and grounded, come back to the moment and focus on what your child is saying, and help them calm down and soothe themselves.

Being a mindful parent can be difficult in the beginning, and the journey is likely not to go smoothly at first. As time passes and you practice more and more, you will find that mindfulness is the best technique for quelling the intensity that can come with ADHD.

# ADHD and Executive Function

Executive function is a phrase that may scare some parents because it can sound incredibly formal and daunting. However, it's simply a cognitive skill that enables humans to plan, organize, prioritize, and complete tasks. In children with ADHD, executive function presents differently and leads to struggles with analyzing, planning, and scheduling. Tasks–especially those on a deadline–can be incredibly difficult for children with ADHD. In children with ADHD, this ability is not absent, but has more difficulty following through, and is called executive dysfunction (Barkley, 2021).

## Executive Function and ADHD

The phrase executive function was conceived by Karl Pribram in the 1970s, when research showed that these functions were managed by the prefrontal cortex. In children with ADHD, the typical path in the brain that certain questions would take simply isn't followed (Barkley, 2021). There are different circuits in the brain responsible for different types of jobs: what, when, why, and who. In a brain with ADHD, these signals may not make it to their destination and thus cause trouble for a child with ADHD.

The "what" brain signal goes from the frontal lobe toward the back of the brain toward the area where "working memory" is stored. This is directly connected with plans, goals, and the future.

The "when" brain signal goes from the prefrontal area of the brain toward the cerebellum at the back of the head. This signal is all about timing and behavior, punctuality, and when we do certain things. This explains why some children with

ADHD may struggle with time management.

The "why" brain signal is the third circuit and comes from the frontal lobe toward the central part of the brain. This is linked with emotions, control of emotions, and emotional intelligence. This is the signal that chooses among multiple options and makes decisions. Without this signal being delivered, tantrums and emotional meltdowns can be common and expected. For a child with ADHD, they may simply not understand their emotions because the brain signal is not following its path to completion.

The final brain circuit is the "who" signal and goes from the frontal lobe to the back of the hemisphere, where self-awareness is located. This is where we are aware of what we do, how we feel, and what is happening to ourselves. A child with ADHD may lack self-awareness and not realize the impact of their actions due to this signal being absent.

It's also important to note that executive function is important to seven specific social skills: self-awareness, inhibition, non-verbal memory, verbal memory, emotional regulation, motivation, and problem solving (Barkley, 2021). Any parent of a child with ADHD already knows that these seven areas of life can be incredibly difficult for their child.

## ADHD and Brain Management Control

Now that we know more about executive function and the role it plays in ADHD in children, we can discuss the brain management and control functions of a child with ADHD. In a study published in The Lancet and financed by the National Institute of Health, 3,000 children and adults were examined using MRI brain scans ("Large-Scale MRI Study," 2017). Slightly more than half of the participants have ADHD. The findings of this research give greater insight into how the brain of a child with ADHD differs from that of a child without ADHD:

- Five of seven areas of the brain were smaller in children with ADHD.
- The region of the brain with the greatest size discrepancy was the amygdala, the area that is most related with emotional and self-control. This area also specializes in the ability to prioritize tasks.
- Regions of the brain linked with learning and memory were also smaller.
- Medications for ADHD are not the culprit for the size discrepancies. Children who are medicated for ADHD exhibited the same size differences in the same

areas as those who never used medication.

- In adults with ADHD, the size discrepancies did not exist. It appears that the size becomes similar between those with ADHD and those without after the teen years.

You may be wondering what these findings mean for you, as a parent. Well, there are a few things we can do with this information.

First, it proves that ADHD is a real brain condition with physical and presentable evidence ("Large-Scale MRI Study," 2017). This, in itself, can be incredibly calming and validating to know that this is not something "made up."

Second, while the brain scans show that children will grow and their brains will get to the appropriate size in the five regions where it may be small, ADHD symptoms will not go away ("Large-Scale MRI Study," 2017). As a lifelong condition, ADHD may require lifelong intervention, therapies, and strategies to assist in treatment.

Third, this study proves that children with ADHD may simply not understand their full range of emotional intelligence or their ability for self-control until they reach a more mature age. This is not to be discouraging, but instead motivational. This is a thread of hope; continue to work with your child on emotional intelligence and self-control. Eventually, they will grasp the concepts well.

## EXERCISES: Reframing the Parental View of Executive Function

Because parenting is already an arduous task, it can be incredibly upsetting to know that there is something going on in your child's brain that you can't quite fix, not that children with ADHD are something to be fixed. However, it can feel that way during times of high stress.

Instead of wallowing helplessly, it is integral to your mindfulness and parenting journeys to reframe the way in which you view Executive Function, your child's ADHD, and the stigma of ADHD. Children with ADHD may already start to wonder what's wrong with them, so getting ahead of these thoughts is ideal. There are two sure-fire ways to reframe your parental view of executive function and ADHD: positive affirmations and structure.

Positive affirmations are essentially a goldmine of positivity. They are something that parents of children with ADHD are in desperate need of. Some of the best positive affirmations are those that bring you to the present moment. These affirmations are a piece of mindfulness and will help assuage those worries and fears that creep in when your thoughts begin to ruminate. Consider making your own affirmations or using some of the following:

- "There is nothing inherently wrong with my child. They have flaws like the rest of us, but they are kind, loving, and good."
- "My child's ADHD does not define them."
- "My child requires my love, patience, and assistance."
- "I am going to model good emotional intelligence for my child by refusing to yell at them for their outbursts."
- "My child is constantly learning, even when they are having a difficult time controlling themselves."
- "ADHD is my beautiful child's superpower!"

Take some time to write your own affirmations, specific to your children and your ADHD experiences. Remember to try and reframe the experience positively, such as, "My child needs a good role model for expressing appropriate emotions," as opposed to, "My child is screaming and I'm going crazy." Reframing the experience into what your child needs works wonders.

The second surefire way to reframe your parental view of ADHD and executive functions is to provide a consistent structure for your child. Children with ADHD typically require more structure than children who do not have ADHD (Orenstein, 2010). A child with ADHD will be more amicable to changing tasks and going throughout their day when they know what to expect and when to expect it. It may not need to be a very strict schedule or followed all the time, but it certainly should be implemented for daily use. Having a routine or structure will help a child with ADHD accept the day ahead with fewer epic meltdowns, especially if there is a small warning ahead of time to let them know the progression of the day.

Take some time to create a routine to help you and your family establish an expectation for your child. Go over the routine with them so they know what is expected of them. Ideally, a routine for the morning (before school, perhaps) and a routine for bedtime are the best ways to ensure quiet and smoother transitions between activities. However, the beginning will be difficult. It may take your child a few days to get the hang of it and patience will serve you well during this time.

## The Challenge of Task Completion

I remember asking my daughter to take a bath five times one afternoon after school only to find her on the floor with her dolls after two hours of my asking. She was quietly fabricating stories with her toys, her clean clothes piled beside her as she played, as if she'd simply gotten side-tracked. Which is exactly what happened. For children with ADHD, focusing, retaining attention, and keeping information are difficult and contribute to the failure to complete a task ("How to Help Your Child," n.d.).

The solution is a touch simple: break the task into a few smaller tasks. Instead of asking my daughter to take a bath after that first mishap, I'd instead ask her to gather her clothes, a much smaller and more easily completed task. Then, I'd ask her to turn the water on. When completed, I'd ask her to gather the toys she'd want to play with in the tub. Finally, when the clothes were gathered, the toys were collected, and the tub was filling, I'd ask her to take a bath. Usually, this was done without fuss or fight.

Try this method yourself and see how small the steps are that your child requires in order to maintain the instruction and follow through with the complete task.

## Mindfulness and Stress

Now that we have discussed ADHD at length and you're now equipped with several strategies to specifically handle your child's ADHD, let's talk about you. Raising your child and handling your child's ADHD might be causing an insurmountable level of stress to build on your shoulders. Using mindfulness, you can keep that stress in check and keep it from pummeling you into the ground.

An archaic method of meditation, mindfulness has been studied by some of the top universities in the world and found to provide assistance with building emotional strength and resilience toward external stressors (Alidina, 2019). Mindfulness means pausing to tap into your own mind and avoid reacting to a situation until you have yourself together. Mindfulness can help you be more in tune with your thoughts, aid in reactions to stress, bring awareness to your needs, bring awareness to your emotions, and foster feelings of compassion inside yourself (Alidina, 2019).

Let's discuss how to quell stress using two mindfulness techniques that are ultimately tried and true: using S.T.O.P. and bringing awareness to your breath.

## EXERCISE: Using S.T.O.P.

S.T.O.P. is an acronym and one of the best mindfulness techniques out there. This is meant for those really intense moments when your child is having an intense meltdown and you simply aren't sure what to do. You might be on the verge of screaming, but it's integral to model emotional intelligence and keep your cool. Using this technique can help you create some mental room for you to ease your worried mind before you tackle the issue (Goldstein, 2013). The acronym means the following:

- Stop
- Take a breath
- Observe
- Proceed

The core principle is to pause and keep from reacting. You'll respond to the external stimuli after you have breathed and observed what is happening in front of you. By using this technique, you'll be able to remain present and handle outbursts with the utmost grace.

## EXERCISE: Awareness of Breath

In a similar vein to S.T.O.P., awareness of the breath is simply the act of pausing for a set amount of time and breathing. It's all about being in the present moment and paying attention to every detail of the air filling your lungs and leaving your lungs.

Get into a comfortable position, ideally in a quiet environment, and focus on being in the moment. Focus on the way the air moves through your body and be mindful of the thoughts coming in and going out of your head.

Do this for any amount of time you'd like; five minutes is the recommended start time.

### Informal Mindfulness

Busy parents, never fear; mindfulness is a technique that can be done during the busiest of days. This is called informal mindfulness. Karen Pace from Michigan State University discusses the differences between formal and informal meditation, saying, "...practices can also be adapted into informal practice...When we practice mindfulness in a more informal way, we are noticing our experience from moment to moment and bringing out attention to one thing as many times as we can throughout the day" (Pace, 2016). This means something as mundane as washing dishes can be a mindfulness exercise if we take time to feel how the soap feels against our skin and how the water feels on our hands. It also means slowing the movements down to truly appreciate every moment of the feeling.

## EXERCISE: Daily Informal Mindfulness

There are dozens of ways to implement informal mindfulness into daily life. Here are several:

- *Walking.* Take careful note of how your body moves when you walk, how your hips, legs, and arms feel.

- *Sitting outside.* Watch nature around you, feel the warmth of the sun on your skin, and notice how the wind feels through your hair.

- *Showering.* Take note of how the soap feels on your body, and how the water feels going over you.

- *Driving.* Carefully pay attention to what you see, how the steering wheel feels in your hands, and the sounds of driving around you.

- *Breathing.* Awareness of the breath can be done anytime, anywhere, even in a crowded place.

## Action Plan: Bringing Awareness to Your Child's ADHD

In this chapter, you have learned a lot about ADHD and mindfulness. You have learned several strategies and techniques on how to carefully and mindfully take care of yourself and your child. You have also learned more about executive function and how to reframe ADHD in your parental viewpoint.

Now, it's time to look ahead. You have a wealth of knowledge about ADHD and how it affects a child; it's time to take that knowledge and spread it. To someone who doesn't know much about ADHD, your child may come across as hyper, unteachable, and incapable of listening. You know better. You know there is a real reason and that your child is completely normal. It's time to spread that knowledge.

By bringing your child's teachers, grandparents, and siblings up to speed on ADHD and how it affects their loved one, you and your support system can work as a team to help your child get the care, patience, and emotional resilience they need. It may not be easy, but you have the mindfulness techniques and strategies to help implement systems to help. Get out there and make sure everyone knows how they can help you as you help your child.

# Why Your Self-Care is Important to Your Child

Raising a child with ADHD is hard. Not a single person can contest that claim. This is why it's so important to take care of yourself. You cannot possibly take care of your child if you cannot first take care of yourself. Think about being on an airplane while the flight attendant is discussing what to do in an emergency. The advice is to always put your mask on before putting one on your child. This is because you are important for your child's safety. You must be there to take care of them, emotionally and physically. That being said, let's get into the impact of ADHD on parents and marriage, and strategies on how to conduct self-care when raising a child with ADHD.

## The Impact of ADHD On Parents

In a study conducted by Dr. V A Harpin at the Ryegate Children's Centre in the United Kingdom, it was discovered that ADHD "may affect all aspects of a child's life" (Harpin, n.d.). In fact, the study goes on to say that parents and siblings are at risk for "disturbances to family and marital functioning" (Harpin, n.d.).

As a child grows, the symptoms of ADHD change and evolve. The aspects of the disorder vary and continue into adulthood with other types of troubles in occupational and personal life.

Parents may have a particularly difficult time finding childcare for young children with ADHD as some family members may not want to care for the child. Parents may also feel discouraged by their child's difficult time in social situations and any difficulties finding friends. Poor sleep patterns with children who have ADHD are common, as well, and can cause an incredibly difficult time for parents who are not getting enough rest as a result (Harpin, n.d.). Additionally, Harpin suggests that parents raising a child with ADHD may struggle to find time to themselves and thus may have strained family relationships, particularly in a marriage (Harpin, n.d.). He also mentions that parents of sixty-six children with ADHD expressed more dissatisfaction in their parenting journey than those of children in a control group (Harpin, n.d.).

Simply put, parenting a child with ADHD is difficult and is associated with a higher level of stress, less sleep, and more difficulty in dealing with emotional outbursts and tantrums.

## EXERCISE: Give Yourself a Break

Because of all the aforementioned troubles that can come with raising a child with ADHD, it's incredibly important to take care of yourself as needed. It's not only for the sake of modeling good self-care habits; sometimes you simply need a moment to yourself.

I'll never forget one night when I was exhausted and basically a zombie. My daughter just couldn't sleep and the extra energy inside her was keeping us both awake. My partner came to me and ushered me into our bedroom. "Do you want control or peace?" he asked me. At the time, it didn't make much sense, but then it dawned on me. I needed to give up the control I was trying to exert by begging my child to simply sleep and accept the break my partner offered me.

It is important to give yourself a break and accept the help as needed. You are a parent, not a machine. Even if you need a five-minute breather alone in the bathroom, take it. You deserve a break– or five–throughout the day!

## Taking Baby Steps Toward Change

You and your family aren't going to be able to make leaps and bounds in one night with any of the goals and changes you wish to make. Instead, it's going to take persistence, time, and patience. In the previous chapter, we discussed employing mindfulness techniques in daily life as well as setting up a structure for your child. Now, we will discuss the need to employ self-care methods throughout the entire journey of raising your child with ADHD. As with all parenting, there will be easy days and there will be hard days. The point of self-care is to build resilience and make yourself more capable of handling difficult times when they arise.

It can be easy to forgo self-care for the sake of your children, but making the change from no-self-care to decent-self-care is vital to your mental health and well-being, not to mention your parenting methods.

Starting the journey to self-care is rife with little steps to take every single day. There are a number of small steps that you can take each day to improve your self-care routine and find time to rebuild your emotional resilience. Here are a few ideas:

- *Taking naps or getting to sleep a little earlier.* I know, sleeping is the antithesis to fun–even as an adult–but sleep is vital to your emotional resilience and your ability to mindfully parent.
- *Exercise daily.* Some parents may actually find exercise incredibly invigorating and beneficial. For others, it may feel more like a chore.
- *Eat healthy foods.* Relying on junk food will only make you feel like junk while eating healthy food can boost emotional resilience.
- *Get outside.* A walk through nature can help reorient someone who has ruminating thoughts, and vitamin D from the sun can help keep depression and anxiety at bay (Scaccia, 2020).
- *Spend time with a pet.* Pets have the ability to boost happiness and offer emotional support to many people.

These are only a few of the small self-care things that can help build emotional resilience. Others can include going out for drinks with friends, engaging in a favorite hobby, or relaxing with a good book.

## EXERCISE: Decluttering

One of the best ways to remain mindful is simply to have less to worry about within the home. With less, you aren't worried about the mess, the clutter, or the stress associated with constantly cleaning. When the area around you feels too messy and cluttered, you may experience difficulty figuring out how to center yourself (Greiner, 2020). Mindfulness can also be practiced while decluttering, as it will bring your mind to the present moment and focus your energy so that you feel like breathing is easier.

While decluttering may not sound like a pinnacle of mindfulness or parenting for

ADHD, it does offer a reprieve from daily stress in small doses. When that kitchen counter is clean, making meals is easier, which can make all the difference during the day.

While decluttering, practice mindfulness by taking a good, slow look at everything you are attempting to declutter. Examine the items with your eyes, with your hands, and with your other senses. Feel the weight of each item as you place it where it belongs in the home. Bring yourself to the present moment and focus on the task at hand without letting your mind wander to other things, like worries, stresses, and anxieties.

## Attention Matters: Do You Also Have ADHD?

While modern medicine isn't exactly aware of the factors that contribute to ADHD, it has come up with a few components that may work together to be responsible. One of those components is a genetic factor. ADHD can run in the family line ("Attention Deficit Hyperactivity Disorder," 2018). Research has indicated that both parents and siblings of a child who has been diagnosed with ADHD do commonly have the disorder themselves. The disorder is complicated, however, and there are other factors at play.

That being said, it's entirely possible that a member of the family may have passed the condition down the line to your child. You and your partner may wish to evaluate yourselves to get more answers and insights into your family. This would also be beneficial for your child as they grow into adulthood.

We've discussed the symptoms of ADHD in children, but we haven't touched on the symptoms in adults. The following list is a compilation of symptoms that some professionals believe are exhibited in adults with ADHD ("Attention Deficit Hyperactivity Disorder," 2018):

- Inattention or nonchalance.
- Picking up new projects without finishing old projects.
- Underdeveloped organizational skills.
- Difficulty with focus and identifying priorities.
- Constantly misplacing things.
- Frequent forgetfulness.

- Trouble with interrupting or remaining quiet for long periods of time. Also, trouble with impulse control when speaking.

- Varying mood swings or an inability to emotionally regulate.

- Difficulty handling stressful situations.

- Intense impatience.

- Engaging in risky activities with little regard for safety measures, such as speeding when driving a car ("Attention Deficit Hyperactivity Disorder," 2018).

If you have noticed your child's ADHD, it's time to look within and see if you exhibit any of the symptoms of ADHD in adults. If this is the case, you may want to pursue medication or therapy treatments to help deal with the disorder. Knowledge is always the first step in creating change. Knowing about your own struggles is also a form of self-care itself, as you will now be armed with the necessary information that will pave the way in helping you take better care of yourself and your mental health.

## EXERCISE: Compile a Behavioral Triage List

Think about your behavior. Do you show any symptoms of ADHD? What types of symptoms do you see in yourself that may coincide with this disorder? It's time to write each of these symptoms down in a bulleted list and examine each one.

Next, you'll take some time going through each symptom, and you'll decide how to best handle your own behaviors. For example, if you feel you're too forgetful, you may want to start carrying around a planner or small notepad to write down important dates and appointments. If you feel that you interrupt too much and get distracted mid-conversation, you'll probably want to remove any potential distractions from the area while having an important conversation.

Write down each symptom and a corresponding solution that you can refer to in a pinch. By doing so, you'll be helping manage your own ADHD symptoms, model good coping strategies for your child with ADHD, and taking care of yourself by giving yourself the attention you deserve to build a better you.

## Self-Care Can Help You Get Unstuck From Stress

Self-care in itself is a form of attention. It's just one that you're giving much needed attention to yourself. Stress can come in many forms and can plague you with worries and woes of a future that has not even happened yet. Pausing and using mindfulness techniques while taking care of yourself can help you get unstuck from the constant pit of anxiety and worry that can drag you down. This means that taking fifteen deep breaths while taking a bath can boost calmness and reduce stress. This is a form of self-care and attention.

Mindfulness is a form of focus and attention that seeks to accept the current moment without judgment or fear, which can ease stress and tension ("Focus More to Ease Stress," 2011). Consider combining self-care techniques with mindfulness to bring attention to your stress and expel it from your day.

## EXERCISE: Paying Attention to Your Stress

It might seem counterintuitive to focus on your stress, but it can be incredibly helpful. Bringing your attention to the issue at hand–whether a tense traffic jam or a problem at work–can help you realize the true weight of the situation. Think about the issue and then imagine it as a helium-filled balloon floating away into the air and popping into the atmosphere.

There is no reason to worry about what you can't change. Let the issue float away from you and then use a mindfulness technique to bring your attention to something else entirely.

## Make Time For Self-Care

Waiting for some time to magically appear in front of you for some downtime will only leave you disappointed. Chances are that time isn't going to come. You'll have to schedule time in your day to allow for self-care. After all, being the last thing on the long list of daily to-do's doesn't feel good; although, you may not realize that if you aren't adequately paying yourself enough attention ("Why You Need to Make Time for Self-Care," n.d.).

By scheduling it, you'll be making yourself a priority and modeling good self-care skills for your children. Without appropriate self-care methods, you may run the risk of "burnout, depression, anxiety, resentment, and a whole host of other negative implications" (Glowiak, 2020).

Instead of waiting, take your planner out and write a chunk of time to dedicate just for you. Or perhaps pull up your digital calendar and allot a time slot dedicated to your own personal care. Whatever method you choose is perfect if it gets you the self-care you need.

## EXERCISE: Focus On the Joy in Life

It can be easy to fall into a pit of despair and focus only on the negative, but this will get you nowhere and will only make your mind a sad and dark place. Instead, engage in some positive affirmations about life that will invoke positivity, love, and hope. Here are a few examples:

- "I deserve to take care of myself and shower myself with nice things."
- "I deserve to be happy and experience calm moments."
- "I adore my child's laugh."
- "I appreciate the fresh air in my lungs and the quiet environment around me."
- "I am excited for the vibrant future ahead of me."

## Action Plan: Caring for the Caregiver

Now that you know how important it is to give yourself time, attention, and care, it's time to make yourself a priority in your action plan. Remember that you are integral to the proper functioning of your family unit and fundamental in your child's ADHD experience. Taking care of yourself means that you can take care of your family. That being said, think about the best ways that you can implement self-care into your day. Is there a specific time of the day that is most ideal? Perhaps a walk or a gym session after your child gets on the bus is the best thing for you. Maybe, you'd rather take a long and luxurious bath with your favorite book after the kids are in bed. Anything that makes you feel refreshed, alive, and ready to handle any stress thrown your way is perfect.

Now, schedule your self-care time each week or more as needed, and you'll start to see an improvement in your emotional resilience in no time.

# Change Begins With You

As the parent of a child with ADHD, you are the ultimate role model. You will be the one to show your child how to express their emotions and how to expand their knowledge of emotional intelligence and resilience. You may feel like it's too hard sometimes to be your child's ultimate source of knowledge about the world. This is why it is so vital to your parenting journey that you make small changes to your own operation in order to provide your child with the proper foundations for their own adult life. In this chapter, we will discuss how to reframe certain viewpoints and offer exercises on how to adopt mindful practices and thought processes that will help your child thrive.

## Reframing Difficult Experiences

A technique called cognitive reframing can help ease some of the frustration you may feel during your parenting journey. "Cognitive reframing is a technique used to shift your mindset so you're able to look at a situation, person, or relationship from a slightly different perspective" (Morin, 2021). When a negative experience happens in life, it can be easy to get caught in a loop of negative thoughts and emotions. It may feel good to ruminate on the issue instead of solving it, but this is not good for anyone. Instead, you'll want to shift your viewpoint so that you are able to see the reality of the situation without your bias.

Reframing your thoughts may be hard, but it simply boils down to how that situation has a silver lining. Instead of thinking about how exhausting it is to handle some of your child's outbursts, you may instead want to view them as learning experiences for your child. When looked at through a lens of positivity, difficult experiences can morph into powerful lessons as opposed to hard realities.

## The Dangers of Compounding Difficult Experiences

Each event is its own experience, in its own bubble of information that should not be compounded with other events. This means that, as a parent, you must manage each huddle as its own unique event without judgment, bias, or prejudice. Maybe your child has spilled juice on the floor for the eighth time this week, but by compounding all eight experiences into one big, messy ball, you'll only feel rising irritation and get yourself worked into a frenzy about the cleaning process.

Instead, it's important to separate and isolate each frustrating experience so that they don't build up into an emotional tower that will eventually collapse from the stress. This may be difficult for some, but try the following mindfulness technique to help the events fizzle away from you and avoid letting that emotional tower build up.

## EXERCISE: Separating Experiences

Sit with your legs crossed, wherever is the most comfortable place for you. Close your eyes and imagine each irritating experience as if it were a bubble. The bubble can begin at your face and begin floating upward until finally it pops and the little particles of it drop to the floor while the air inside goes up toward the sky.

Imagine the air inside of the bubble is the frustrating experience you've had. Let it go up and dissipate into the atmosphere away from you. Let it leave you in peace and harmony as you remain grounded. By imagining this, you can let go of the experience and separate yourself from the frustration. Do this with each individual experience, being sure not to compound them. When you are done, slowly open your eyes, take a deep breath, and continue your day with a calmer mindset.

## Seizing the Reins

Making little changes is all about a sense of control. No one else can cause little changes in your life besides yourself. You have the power to build the life, family, and world you wish to live in. By employing the small methods outlined in this chapter, you're one step closer to taking the reins of your life and directing your world instead of following the path laid out for you. Remember that you are in control of your life even if you can't control every aspect of life or other people in your life (Williamson, 2021). Use the following affirmations to remind yourself that you are in control of your life and motivate you:

- "I choose the best path for me."
- "I may not be able to control everything, but I control how I respond and react to things."
- "I am learning new ways to change and adapt every day."
- "I can breathe through challenges and emotions without losing my cool."
- "I deserve to build a world I'm proud to live in."

## EXERCISE: Fifteen Breaths

Mindful breathing is a great way to build up emotional flexibility and reduce the effects of stress and anger ("Mindful Breathing," n.d.). This exercise is done by focusing on the way the air enters and exits your lungs for fifteen consecutive breaths. During particularly stressful moments, you may want to take a larger breath in for three seconds, hold that breath for two seconds, and exhale through the mouth for four seconds ("Mindful Breathing," n.d.). If you are not feeling overly stressed, you may want to simply examine each breath as it comes into you and leaves you, focusing all your attention away from the current stressor.

## Fostering Independence and The Executive Function Toolkit

Cultivating independence can be a difficult job for a parent. The desire for independence begins rather young in children. At around first and second grade, children desire to choose their own clothing, walk home from the bus stop alone, or go to bed at a later time (Anthony, n.d.). Some changes will be appreciated by you but others might make you feel like you're going to rip your hair out. Some of the decisions your child wants to make will have you tugging at your hair in frustration and make you extra cautious as you watch your child venture through life.

Around the age of seven, children can think more abstractly and make rational judgments. They also learn more about the value of pros and cons, actions, and causes and effects, which are all skills integral to fostering independence (Anthony, n.d.). As previously mentioned, a lot of these abstract concepts, like emotional regulation and self-control, are difficult for children with ADHD to cultivate. At around age seven, these skills develop across the board and executive functions may begin to improve remarkably.

Another note to add by an author for Scholastic, Michaelle Anthony, is that the U.S. Department of Education states that children have peak performance when they have strong parental connections while expressing differing viewpoints (Anthony, n.d.). Parents are vital to the independence of a child and a cornerstone to fall back on when emotions run high.

All of this information on independence is fundamental to the toolkit you will want to create for the improvement of executive functioning in your child with ADHD. This toolkit will be beneficial for a child as young as four–the age at which symptoms begin to arise–and can be used throughout the entirety of adolescence. It can also be modified as needed. Because some of the main issues for children with ADHD are working memory, emotional regulation, and task completion, the toolkit includes the following:

- *Coping activities for outbursts and emotional turmoil.* Many children may find it difficult to keep themselves under control when they have ADHD and intense emotions. By first validating and accepting those emotions, children can then move on to distracting themselves from the pain with a separate activity.

- *Practicing gratitude and positive affirmations.* By practicing gratitude with your child, you can make them more aware of the good things in their life to focus on, as opposed to the negative. Positive affirmations can boost their self-esteem and quell the concerns they may have about their condition.

- *Giving your child choices throughout the day.* Letting your child pick out their school clothes, their snack, or which video game they want to play during their allotted screen time can be a great way to quell outbursts and make them feel like they have a say in what happens to them. It will also make them feel like they have control over their lives and their body.

- *Encourage your child to ask for help.* A child with ADHD may find it difficult to get tasks done and then get incredibly frustrated at any roadblocks in their path. Allow them the space to try things on their own but also encourage them to ask for a helping hand when necessary.

## Perfection is a Thief of Happiness

Striving to be the perfect parent and raise the perfect children will only set you up for incredible and heartbreaking disappointment. Not only will being a perfectionist stress you out but it will be harmful to the well-being of your child. A perfectionist mindset–and the stress and anxiety that comes with it–is not something you would want modeled for your child, so it is integral to refrain from modeling this type of behavior. Instead, you will want to find a good middle ground in which your child can thrive;one where they are not burdened by the need for things to be perfect and know when they need to rest.

There are many signs that signal you are expecting too much from yourself as a parent (Morin, 2021). These include:

- Frequent criticisms of yourself.
- Placing blame on yourself when your child does something wrong.
- Comparing your parenting journey to others and feeling like you don't meet the standard.
- Constantly beating yourself up for not doing more with or for your child, regardless of how much you do.
- Second-guessing your choices as a parent.
- Resorting to yelling or screaming as a result of your impossible-to-meet standards.
- There are also many signs that indicate your expectations for your child are too high and that you are seeking perfection from them (Morin, 2021). These include:
- Having a hard time observing your child do something incorrectly.
- Constant micromanaging as your child works on something.
- Pressuring your child to perform without flaw.
- Encouraging your child to pursue your dreams, not their own.
- Placing all your self-esteem and self-worth on your child's success.
- Viewing your child's normal activities as if they are life-altering experiences.

Children,and parents, for that matter, cannot thrive in an environment where the standards are unattainable. It's time to let go of perfection and let things go as they may. Next, we will discuss an exercise to help ease the perfectionism burden and allow you to simply exist in the present moment.

## EXERCISE: Watch the Weather

In this exercise, you'll want to grab a drink of your choice and take a seat near a window or outside, wherever comfortable. A seat on the porch, in the house within view of the outside world, or on the lawn are preferable. Ideally, you'll want to be able to feel the sun on your skin. Next, you'll simply bring your focus to the weather outside, watching as the cloud cover interrupts the sunshine or how the rain sounds as each drop hits the concrete sidewalk outside. The idea during this time is to bring your attention specifically to the weather and avoid letting your mind wander. If it wanders, you might get swept away in a sea of emotions or anxiety. Remember: anxiety is the act of living in a future that hasn't happened yet. This exercise seeks to avoid getting lost in the cycle of living in the future that hasn't happened yet, the millions of "what-if" scenarios, and the fear of the unknown.

Spend fifteen minutes simply watching the weather and try to observe things you may never have noticed before while keeping your focus on the present. This exercise is ideal for people who enjoy the sunshine or the rain, both of which can be calming.

## The Rippling Effect of ADHD

Researcher Judith Wiener discusses the ripple effect of ADHD in her study published by Sage Journals: "Adolescents with attention-deficit/hyperactivity disorder (ADHD) are highly vulnerable. Although their hyperactive symptoms tend to decrease from childhood through adolescence, their inattentive symptoms remain stable. Their academic, social, and emotion regulation difficulties persist and they are at risk for co-occurring oppositional defiant disorder, conduct disorder, anxiety, and depressive disorders" (2020). The effects of ADHD, essentially, ripple throughout the child's entire life and support system. Wiener mentions that self-perception and relationships inside and outside the home are of particular risk for the rippling effect. Trouble with academic and behavioral issues is not dismissed from the argument.

While this may sound like a bad thing, it's not entirely terrible news when a child knows how to manage their ADHD symptoms. The key to handling this rippling effect is love, attention, and fulfilling the emotional and mental needs a child may have. This means having less pressure placed on them to be perfect and understanding their emotions, actions, and consequences for behavior.

# EXERCISE: Reframe the Parental View On Academic Challenges

Many parents may have a difficult time letting go of the need for their child to be a perfect student, but this is entirely unnecessary. Academics may play a large role in your child's life, but the mental and emotional well-being of a child is much more important than their academic performance. The stress and emotional exhaustion of getting perfect grades can be almost too much for a child with ADHD ("Emotional Health," n.d.).

Thus, it's time to use positive affirmations to reframe the way that you may view your child's grades and the priority you place on their academic achievement. These affirmations should focus on the positive side or silver lining of a situation. Here are a few examples of silver linings and positive affirmations you may want to adopt:

- "My child's health matters more than their academic performance. If they are exhausted, they need rest first."

- "I can help my child find a way to understand the material better through online or tutoring resources."

- "My words, attitude, and actions impact my child more than I know; I have the power to encourage them to be positive and take it slow when they need to" ("Emotional Health," n.d.).

Keep in mind that a child with ADHD may have a harder time focusing and will stumble through a lot of their academic life. This is not uncommon or unusual and will require a lot of patience from you, the parent. However difficult, it is possible for your child to succeed in academics, although it may not be the way you envisioned it.

Have patience with your child and remember to keep your focus on the positive to reframe your view.

## Action Plan: Externalize

Now that we realize that a lot of small pieces of the puzzle begin with you, you can move on to making sure that all the little stressors in life don't remain locked up inside your chest and foster negativity.

Instead, engage in the fifteen breaths and watch the weather exercises to release the negative experiences and let them drift away from you. Start each new day from scratch, knowing that it will never be a carbon copy of the one before it. Use breathing, mindfulness, and reframing techniques to reassure yourself that things don't have to build and bubble up inside you and that you can instead let go of negative mindsets. By doing so, you will build a healthier and happier environment in which your child can thrive, regardless of their ADHD diagnosis.

# Communication and Mindfulness for ADHD

When raising a child with ADHD, you may find yourself repeating your words much more often than you want, or feel like you need to. This is incredibly common when communicating with children who have ADHD. While it may be frustrating and difficult to manage, communication can be fostered in healthy ways using behavioral training, positive rewards, and open dialogue. In this chapter, we will discuss the science behind ADHD and communication, as well as offer techniques on how to foster mindfulness in your parenting style in regard to your child's communication trouble.

## How ADHD Impacts Communication

The underlying issue with communication and ADHD is that ADHD "represents a deficit in executive function, a skill set that includes attention, impulse control… and far more. [ADHD is] seen as a disorder of self-regulation" (Bertin, 2014). Thus, children with ADHD may experience language delays in early childhood and suffer from frequent distractibility, interrupting, and trouble with listening to "rapidly-spoken language" (Bertin, 2014).

This doesn't mean that your child is without hope! Using behavioral training methods, even children as young as four can experience growth and development in their communication skills. This is not to say that your child will be a master communicator within a year from the beginning of therapy; the change will be slow, but incredibly beneficial as children grow and develop using positive habits.

## Finding the Middle Ground

Having a conversation with another person is typically an exchange in which two people listen and speak in an alternating pattern. When it comes to holding a conversation with a child with ADHD, alternating patterns do not exist. It can be difficult for them to wait their turn to speak and they often get distracted by other thoughts. The middle ground between complete conversational chaos and control lies with redirection. When your child goes on a tangent a touch too long, it's okay to gently reel them back into the topic at hand.

For example, if you and your child are having a conversation about puppies and your child goes on a branching tangent conversation, you can simply say, *"Let's finish this conversation before we start a new one."* You may even want to add, *"There's more about puppies that I want to say. Is it okay if we finish this topic first and then you can choose the next topic?"* This has a three-fold benefit of reeling your child back into the conversation, giving them a measure of control by allowing them to pick the next topic, and modeling better communication habits for them to use in the future.

## EXERCISE: Tally Talking Time

An effective strategy for helping a child with ADHD and communication trouble help reorient their conversational technique is to allow them to speak and tally up the exchanges you and your child have. This means that every time your child speaks, they get a tally, and every time you speak, you get a tally. At the end of the conversation, you both will compare the tally marks together to make sure there is an equal amount. If the tallies are particularly uneven, in favor of your child's side, you can discuss with them that it's important to listen to other people and hear others' thoughts as well as express their own.

Using tally marks, you can help your child understand their impact on a conversation and how important it is to hear other perspectives.

## Actions vs Words: Helping Your Child Repair Communication Flaws

All development requires action. Research from The University of Waterloo in Canada has shown that children with ADHD may have a much harder time to consider other perspectives compared to children without ADHD ("Studies Link ADHD," n.d.). This study showed that ADHD and communication issues are directly linked and that children with ADHD struggle to understand another person's viewpoint during a conversation.

Therefore, discussing different perspectives and trying to understand the world outside your child's own viewpoint may not click with them. Instead, you'll want to take action. Here are some practices you and your family can take to help your child understand other viewpoints:

- When your child states you are not listening to them, pause. Take time to listen to them speak and let them know that you have stopped, listened, and understand their perspective. De-escalate the situation by letting them know you hear them. This is not to change your mind on the conversation, but to model the idea that you–and they–can accept that other perspectives exist.

- Make a chart. Some children with ADHD learn better with hands-on activities or with visual aids. A chart depicting a staircase, ladder, or sidewalk can illustrate the steps in a conversation and the different stages of communicating.

- Make a rhyme out of it. Children as young as three can learn rhymes and commit them to memory. A rhyme might be just the thing to make your child remember that they must be kind and consider other perspectives.

- Practice asking how your child feels; then, ask your child to inquire about your feelings. This can help your child get into the habit of seeing how other people feel and take those feelings into consideration.

## EXERCISE: Celebrate Communication Success

When your child has done something particularly wonderful and surprising regarding their ADHD symptoms, you must celebrate their success. This will incentivize future communication changes. The more you celebrate your child's success, the more they will strive for the parental approval you give them. Here are some appropriate and healthy ways to celebrate your child's success:

- Take them out for ice cream.

- Go outside and play catch with them.

- Play their favorite video game with them.

- Instill a material reward system, in which they can choose an item from a box of physical toys, stickers, or trinkets.

- Allow them extra screen time on their favorite game, app, or show.

Ideally, whenever your child shows success and achievement in a conversation, you will want to reward them accordingly. You won't, however, want to give them too big of a reward for minor achievements, as they may get too used to how easy it is to gain a reward and might reduce the effort they put in.

Also, make sure you are giving them high-fives, hugs, and positive words of love and affirmation. Affection is crucial for a child, and children with ADHD tend to feel unloved, unwanted, and excluded due to some of the behavior they exhibit. Parental affection can go a long way in reducing these emotions and making them feel loved and supported while they adjust their behaviors.

## Mindfulness and Communication

Mindfulness is about pausing and paying attention to the present and current moment. By doing so, you can identify personal traits that you want to grow within yourself and habits you'd like to expel. Regarding communication, mindfulness means having awareness and handling responses appropriately. This means moving out of autopilot and taking control of yourself before responding. This can be difficult in a heated conversation or debate, but it is an infinitely better solution than resorting to screaming and yelling. By pausing to understand your own reactions, you'll be better able to understand why you feel this way. There could be a multide of reasons you reacted in the way you did; whether you simply woke up cranky, are focusing too much on the past, or find yourself lost in your thoughts. To have a mindful conversation, you'll want to have awareness of your thoughts, emotions, physical sensations, and your body language (Bertin, 2016). Bring yourself an understanding of these aspects of your body before you continue the conversation.

When you bring yourself awareness of what is truly happening inside you, you can handle a conversation with your child in a more measured and productive way.

## EXERCISE: Imagine Communicating Advice to Friends

One of the best exercises to do when struggling with one of your problems is to imagine what you would say to your friend if they were having this issue. Sometimes we can be too hard on ourselves and set our expectations too high.

Instead, pull yourself out of the situation and imagine one of your friends telling you how they are suffering with this issue. Likely, the advice you administer during this imaginary conversation is what you believe you should do.

Trust yourself and listen to the advice you give without any bias that comes from within.

## EXERCISE: What's Your Communication Style?

It is integral to know what your communication style is and how that affects the way you and your child with ADHD communicate together. There are four styles and they operate in starkly different manners:

- *Passive*. This communication style is marked by indifference and constant yielding to others ("4 Types," 2018). If there was a style for doormat, the passive style would be it. The passive types usually do not engage outwardly in communication but instead remain silent and let anger and resentment build inside them. These communicators typically don't make eye contact, have poor posture, and have difficulty saying "no." They also have notoriously poor self-esteem and self-trust.

- *Aggressive*. Aggressive communicators speak in booming and demanding voices while maintaining excessive eye contact. These communicators tend to dominate conversations, projects, and are often controlling. They may also blame, intimidate, and criticize others often. While they can be good leaders and get things done quickly, they can be commanding, rude, and may have trouble listening to others.

- *Passive-Aggressive*. Of all the communication styles, passive-aggressive is the most toxic and uncomfortable. These communicators are passive on the surface but have such intense build ups of emotions that they often spill out in the most inappropriate places. These communicators often gossip about others, mutter under their breath, and use facial expressions that don't link with what they are saying. These types lack open communication and are prone to silent treatments and sabotaging others.

- *Assertive*. Of these four types, assertive is the most beneficial and effective type. In this communication style, a person is able to effectively state what they need, isn't afraid to speak up, and cooperates well with others. These types express their needs, desires, ideas, and feelings while being considerate of others. These communicators have one goal: to have win-win situations in which there is a good balance of good and bad for everyone. Assertiveness strives to take ownership of feelings and behavior without blame and without letting those emotions control their actions.

## Action Plan: Practice Mindful Communication

Now that you know how difficult communication can be for your child and their ADHD symptoms, you'll want to set realistic expectations. Your child will not be a master communicator in a few months or years. Instead, this is a lifelong journey toward self-improvement and executive function development. It will take plenty of effort and time.

Remember to employ mindfulness exercises, including S.T.O.P. and fifteen breaths from a previous chapter, as well as tallying up your talking time and giving advice in your head to sort through difficult challenges. By using these methods, you can keep your cool while helping your child develop their communication skills.

# Using Targeted Praise and Rewards for Success

In the previous chapter, we discussed using praise and rewards for conversational and behavioral success in communication. In this chapter, we will expand on this idea and discuss how this method can dispel negative behavior while incentivizing the adoption of positive behaviors. By employing these methods, you can show your child that you love them, appreciate them, and want the best for them in life.

## Behavioral Training & Reward Systems

A reward and praise approach to handling ADHD is not new; you may have even stumbled across this method in one of countless parenting books. Schools tend to use this method to incentivize positive behaviors, as well. The way behavioral training works is that positive or desired behaviors are rewarded immediately while negative behaviors receive immediate consequences (Low, 2020). Without discouraging negative behaviors, you run the risk of your child falling off track and misremembering the desired behaviors and modifications.

The way this system works is in three easy steps (Low, 2020):

1. *Determine which behaviors should be modified.* In this step, you'll want to specifically name which behaviors you want to eliminate and define target behaviors to replace this negative behavior (Low, 2020). For example, a child who insults other children's art frequently may only be rewarded when they praise another child's art.

2. *Install a system of rewards as a result of good behavior.* In some cases, a tier list may be required here in which the value of the reward is comparable to the value of the action. Little actions may elicit little rewards while bigger actions can elicit bigger rewards. Regardless of the reward, your child must find the reward motivating enough.

3. *Stay with the program. Consistency is key.* It is important for your child to develop the positive habit of the modified behavior. Without a consistent application of the plan, the rewards may have little or no impact and the negative behaviors may not change in the long-term.

Using these three steps, you and your family can find peace, happiness, and modified behavior that empowers your child.

## EXERCISE: Keep a Gratitude Journal

This exercise can be done alone or with your child. If you think your child would benefit from naming a few things they are grateful for, you can ask them to do it with you. This mindfulness technique is meant to pull you from stress and anxiety and bring you to the present moment. The idea is simple: think of five things you are grateful for in that moment. These things can be the weather, the air you breathe, the food you eat, your child's laugh, or your relationship with your partner. Try to phrase these gratitudes in a complete sentence that illustrates why you are grateful for that thing or person. For example, instead of writing "I am grateful for my child," consider writing "I am grateful for my child's curiosity and ingenuity." By identifying the specific parts of your child that make you grateful, you can boost your gratitude and overall happiness.

Try writing at least five things to be grateful for every day to boost gratitude and positive thinking.

## EXERCISE: Establishing a Reward System

It may take you extra time to establish a reward system that works for your child, as it may be hard to procure rewards, think of rewards that will motivate your child, or make a tier list for different rewards. For example, you may want to assign different positive behaviors with different corresponding rewards. For example, children who don't particularly enjoy washing dishes may be incentivized with larger rewards or more desired rewards. Considering making a tier list like the following (or modify the following to fit your needs):

- Desired Uncommon Behaviors

  - Sharing toys

  - Self-soothing tantrums (and not screaming)

  - Walking away from stressors and fights with siblings

    - Incentives: A trip to the park, baking cookies with mom or dad, a trip to the ice cream parlor or skating rink

- Desired Common Behaviors

  - Doing the dishes

  - Vacuuming the rug

  - Putting away laundry

    - Incentives: A whole sticker sheet, fifteen minutes of playtime outside, extra screen time

- Desired Frequent Behaviors

  - Helping a sibling with something

  - Saying kind words to someone

  - Doing something when asked the first time

    - Incentives: A toy, trinket, sticker from the reward box

Remember that while giving the incentive to your child, it is vital to explain to them why they received the incentive and what behavior you expect to see in the future. Also give them a high-five, hug, or kiss on the cheek to show them how much you appreciate their hard work and love them.

## Using Mindfulness in Praise & Rewards

Now that we've discussed how praises and rewards work, we can touch on employing mindfulness in the process. Mindfulness, as previously mentioned, is about being present in the current moment. As such, you can employ mindfulness in your praises and reward system by simply shoving everything aside and focusing on the here and now.

Consider taking a deep breath before retrieving the reward box in order to ground yourself in the present moment, and letting your awareness rest solely on the breath in your lungs. When you feel grounded, go ahead and grab the reward options.

Focus on the way your child lights up as they choose a toy from the reward box, observe the way the toys feel in your hand as you shuffle through them, and notice the things that your child is most interested in. Keeping your focus on this moment can help you observe what your child likes the most from the box and what you should replenish the box with, as well.

When your child has picked a toy, focus on the weight of the box, the sounds and words your child says as they walk away with the toy, and how you feel watching your child learn.

When you feel grounded and calm, you can resume your normal activities feeling much more rested and at ease in the present time.

## Cut Yourself Some Slack

There will be moments in which you forget to give your child their incentive for a job well-done. There will also be times in which you feel so utterly swamped with work, home, or school stuff that you forget to give your child a high-five. You aren't the only busy parent in the world, and it's entirely reasonable that some rewards will slip through the cracks.

Beating yourself up for missing a reward, falling out of the habit, or forgetting to replenish the reward box will do nothing for you or your child. Instead, cut yourself the slack your deserve and work toward getting back on track. Your energy is better spent getting back to your child's care and behavioral development than beating yourself up. Remember that perfectionism is the thief of happiness. If you've forgotten a reward, praise and affection can substitute in the meantime; give your child a random high-five, hug, or kiss on the head to make sure they know they haven't been forgotten and reassure them that you will always come back for them and their success.

## EXERCISE: Give Yourself a Much-Needed Break

Breaks are necessary, especially when attempting to adopt new mindsets and behaviors. You can easily get emotionally and physically drained from the demands of keeping up with behavior training and employing mindfulness throughout the day. When this emotional drainage occurs, it's time to take a step back and let yourself have a break. This may mean asking your parents or partner to take over the behavior training for a day or two while you collect yourself. There's no shame in pausing to take care of yourself. Consider taking a warm bath, reading a nice book, or going out for some much-needed time alone.

## Action Plan: Focus on Positives in Behavioural Planning

Behavioral training can be difficult, but by using mindfulness to keep yourself grounded, the battle is already half-won. Make sure that you are giving yourself just as much praise as you are showering your child with. You deserve all the encouragement, just as your child does. Stick to the plan and give yourself a break, as needed.

# How to Handle Difficult Behaviors

It is not uncommon for children with ADHD to struggle with emotional maintenance and control. Frequently, children with ADHD tend to have defiant and combative behaviors, which can manifest in a multitude of ways ("Does ADHD Raise the Risk," n.d.). Often, challenging behaviors will include emotional outbursts, the chronic refusal to follow an instruction from a parent or teacher, and distaste for doing things that they know they struggle with. Transitions are particularly hard for children with ADHD, and they may start acting out when asked to do certain things like stop playing, do their school work, or get ready for bed ("Does ADHD Raise the Risk," n.d.).

However difficult, these behaviors can be tamed, modified, and handled in various ways, especially by employing mindfulness and mindful approaches to parenting. We have discussed employing a reward system with your child, which can be a great first step in behavior modification. Next, we will discuss how to further modify behavior by creating boundaries and modifying behaviors that cross over the line.

## Building a Foundation and Creating Boundaries

A foundation for behavior expectations is a perfect start to fostering a healthy connection between your child and the world. This means you'll want to show your child what they can reasonably expect from the world around them and how they are expected to act in the world, as well. For example, teaching your child that they cannot have their sister's new birthday toy simply because they want it is a good place to start. Children with ADHD may not understand what the big deal is and why they can't have their sister's toy, but explaining it to them, regardless of their understanding at the current moment, can help them understand later on. The more you give them the explanation, the more they will understand it later. Each time you see your child expressing intense emotions about something unreasonable, you may want to pull them aside and try to explain the limits and boundaries of the situation they are in. You may get frustrated about their seeming lack of understanding, but these explanations will click eventually.

Often, neurologists and medical professionals will suggest that you and your child begin a behavioral therapy regimen to assist with your child's ADHD-related behavioral issues. For preschool aged children, a lot of this therapy is more focused on giving parents the tools and techniques to help handle difficult behaviors that may otherwise drive both parent and child crazy. The two different types of training through these therapy sessions are Parent-Child Interaction Therapy (PCIT) and Parent Management Training (PMT), both of which have a myriad of benefits that can help both parent and child ("Does ADHD Raise the Risk," n.d.). The following list describes the benefits of these therapy methods and how they can help your child manage themselves and help you handle their difficult behaviors:

- Increased awareness of positive child behaviors that can be rewarded, if the family is using a reward system.

- Instilling the idea that minor misbehaviors should be ignored.

- The training necessary to keep consistent with consequences for major behavioral issues or aggressive acts.

- PMT focuses more on helping the parent develop specific skills related to a child's behavior.

- PCIT revolves more around the interaction between child and parent while the therapist acts as a mediator and evaluates which skills to develop for their communication and growth together.

- Both PMT and PCIT have been noted to decrease negative behaviors in children, such as disruptiveness, belligerence, and defiance ("Does ADHD Run the Risk," n.d.).

- Parents who engage in either type of therapy program have indicated a lowered level of stress and improved relationship with their child.

Discussing boundary-setting in these therapy sessions can give you and your family a clearer idea of how to handle challenging behaviors and develop a more personalized approach to your child's care.

One more way to set boundaries with your child is to make clear and precise schedules and routines for them to follow. Discuss these schedules and routines with your child and make sure they understand any rules, such as "no sugar an hour before bed" or "no TV time until your teeth are brushed." Test out the routines for a few days and don't be afraid to modify them, as needed. Sometimes, a routine simply will not work for you and there's nothing wrong with switching it up a little.

As with anything, there can be obstacles to creating your foundation for boundaries and setting these boundaries can be present. Common obstacles with setting boundaries can include not following through or a lack of consistency. These two obstacles are the biggest and often contribute to a backslide in progress. By giving up on the plans you make and not following through–or only following through sometimes–you run the risk of confusing your child and making it hard for them to understand what is expected of them. Steer clear of these two major pitfalls and stick to your plan to make it serve your family well!

## How to Modify Behavior: Time-Outs

One of the most tried and true methods of discipline for a child is the classic time-out. This method is one of the most used for younger children. For children with ADHD, a time-out is more than a disciplinary method; it can be considered a method of self-care for your child. Things can get very stressful or over-stimulating for a child with ADHD and by removing them from the situation and placing them in a calmer and more manageable environment, they may be able to calm down faster, easier, and with much greater ease than if they were still exposed to the stressful event, person, or environment. After an episode of undesirable behavior, a time-out should be immediately employed and should last only one minute per age of your child. For example, a seven-year-old would have a seven-minute time-out.

After some repetition, your child will come to understand that this consequence will happen when their behavior is unacceptable and can serve as a reminder to not behave in a particular way.

## Grocery Store Meltdowns: What To Do

Sometimes, no matter what you do, you will still have to deal with the classic grocery-store meltdown, especially if your child is under the age of five and has ADHD. While completely expected, it can be incredibly stressful for you, as the parent, to watch your beautiful child pounding their fists on the shelves, throwing something in anger, or kicking their feet on the floor because you won't get them a toy they want.

That being said, the first thing you'll have to do is take a deep breath. Every time you have witnessed a child throwing the same type of tantrum that your own child is throwing, you have likely never passed judgment, made a remark, or thought anything negative (aside from, perhaps, "Thank God, that's not my child"). Remember that no one is judging you, thinking you're a bad parent, or paying much attention to your situation at all, for that matter.

When you've come to terms with this, calmly remove your child from the stressful situation. A trip to the bathroom might help as it can be quieter. Perhaps, you'd rather leave your cart in a place you remember and take your child to the car. This is even more effective if you have a partner available to assist with shopping or discipline.

When your child has been removed from the stressful situation, give them some time to quietly calm down. This may take several minutes for them to fully relax. At that time, explain to them why you removed them from the store and what you expect from them and their behavior. An apology may be required if hurtful words were said by either parent or child. Discuss with your child ways that you both think they can keep from having emotional meltdowns and try using these methods the next time a meltdown occurs. You may, however, have to pull your child out of the grocery store on multiple occasions if they're still under the age of five or six, as they may not fully understand what they are doing wrong.

## EXERCISE: Ground Yourself

Grounding yourself is an incredibly important step in making sure that you don't overreact when your child is in the throes of a meltdown. Instead, you'll want to wait until after you've grounded yourself before responding to the stress. This can feel difficult at first, but when you have practiced grounding techniques enough, you'll be able to do it without thinking twice. Here is a list of grounding techniques that will help you respond rather than react to an ADHD-related meltdown:

- *Bring awareness to yourself, your name, your age, and where you are.* By bringing focus to yourself, you can help alleviate the stress you are feeling from your child's behavior.

- *Take fifteen slow and intentional breaths.* Focus your energy on the breath in your lungs and how they feel entering and exiting your body.

- *Drink cold water or wash your face with cold water.* Water is notoriously helpful for bringing the mind to the present moment. The method of consuming water you choose doesn't matter as long as it works to help your heart rate slow and your stress level come down. Some people prefer to rinse their wrists in cool water.

- *Focus on the words on a poster or item.* By reading something, even if it is meaningless to you, you can bring your mind to the present moment and focus on something that isn't the thing bringing stress to your body.

- *Bring your attention to five things you can see, hear, touch, or smell.* If your child is having a meltdown, you may want to go with five things you can smell or see to turn your attention away from the stress you may be feeling from the tantrum. List those five things in your head before bringing yourself back to the issue at hand.

Use these grounding techniques to bring awareness to yourself and remain calm before handling your child's difficult behaviors.

## EXERCISE: Mindfully Setting Boundaries

This exercise is all about making a list in a mindful state. You may want to wait until your child is tucked into bed at night to make this list, as you will have more uninterrupted time to mindfully think about which boundaries should be listed.

First, use one or more of the aforementioned grounding techniques until you are in a state of calm and peace. When you are fully aware of your calmness, your breath, and your state of contentment, turn your mental attention to the memories of your child's behavior and the areas in which they have crossed boundaries with you. This could be something like not knocking before opening the door, or something as severe as pushing their sibling during an argument. Write down as many behaviors you can remember and what boundaries they crossed. Things like aggression, violence, and name-calling are common boundaries in a family and a good place to start.

If you start to feel yourself get frustrated with the memories, do another grounding technique to remain calm.

When you have your list, you can work toward creating a defined plan of which behaviors are the highest priority for modification and which behaviors can be ignored. You may also want to create a list of rewards that your child might receive for going a certain amount of time without a meltdown or for expelling a negative behavior for a certain period of time.

## The Wings That Make Mindfulness

Cindy Ricardo, from A Caring Counselor blog, discusses that the two wings of mindfulness can be summed up into two concepts: wisdom and compassion (Ricardo, n.d.). If mindfulness were a bird, one wing would include insight, thought, and observation– all things that would make up the concept of wisdom. The other wing would include compassion, intention, relaxation, calmness, and loving-kindness (Ricardo, n.d.). The idea here is that there is a balance between seeing and observing a situation and looking at that same situation with love and calmness. Ricardo states, "There must be a balance between compassion and wisdom, to help us stay present with the challenges we face in life, and to learn from them" (Ricardo, n.d.).

Looking at your parenting journey for your child with ADHD can require a lot of patience and loving-kindness. You may want to use this metaphor during your child's next meltdown or difficult behavior and first observe their actions before applying a very thick layer of loving-kindness to the way they are feeling. Look at your child's actions by balancing like a bird's wings in the wind by saying: "Yes, I see my child having a temper tantrum, but they are feeling strong emotions and need help getting used to them."

When you change your perspective toward kindness and love, you will see your child coming to you with their needs more often and with greater respect.

## Action Plan: Ways To Address a Future Behavioral Crisis

Now that we have discussed challenging behaviors, it's time to formulate a plan to put your new information into practice. Remember to make a list of your child's most disruptive or high-priority behaviors that tend to cross the boundaries in your home. Now, using those behaviors, discuss consequences, schedules, and routines with your child. Clearly, and lovingly, discuss your expectations of them and their behaviors while being realistic that there will be hiccups along the road to developing and modifying behavior.

Laying the foundations for your child's behavior will take time and energy, but these boundaries will serve your child well in the coming years. Don't forget to ground yourself during the process and respond rather than react to their tantrums. Remember: this, too, shall pass.

# Education and ADHD

It's no secret that children with ADHD tend to struggle with academic performance a little more than their peers. The symptoms of their disorder tend to make it harder for them to focus, sit still, and control their impulses. This can mean that children with ADHD might interrupt a lot during lessons, fidgeting with their hands and feet, or get up and walk around when they aren't supposed to. There are options to help children with ADHD thrive academically. Much of this help can be from you, their parents.

## Executive Function, School Performance, and Policy

As discussed earlier in this book, executive function include several key features in decision-making, including the ability to pay attention, achieve mental flexibility, the ability to control impulses, and "working memory, [which is] a temporary storage system in the brain that holds several facts or thoughts in mind while solving a problem or performing a task" (Low, 2020). As such, school performance can be deeply impacted in children with ADHD since they will have a harder time with some–or all–aspects of executive function.

As a child grows and matures, some of these symptoms may be easier to handle, especially with medication as needed. There may be run-ins with school policies, however, that require sitting still for long periods of time. The best thing to do is discuss your child's ADHD diagnosis with a representative or guidance counselor at the school your child attends. "To meet the needs of children with ADHD, schools can be part of effective treatment plans for children with ADHD; and provide special education services or accommodations" ("ADHD and School Changes," n.d.). This means that a school can participate in your child's special accommodations for attention, whether this means a smaller class, special one-on-one education, or extra materials.

As children approach high school, there may be a higher demand for attention and impulse control. Fidget toys can help, as long as they are quiet. ADDitude Magazine discusses how children can stay focused on classwork:

- Use colored pencils or highlighters to organize notes.
- Review notes as often as possible.
- Quietly multitask during class, if needed. Sometimes, there's nothing wrong with doodling during a lecture.
- Break large tasks into smaller ones. Instead of thinking of it as a five-page essay, think of it as a one-page essay that you have to do five times. This might make it feel more manageable.

## Create an Educational Plan and Influence the System

"The best approach considers each child's strengths and vulnerabilities, as well as each individual family's needs and functioning" (Calderon, 2020). With the help of your child's school and your own intuition, your family can create an educational plan that can work well for your child and share that plan with other parents of children with ADHD to help them, too. It may be hard at first, but by using trial and error, as well as helping other parents in your position, you can make the school system more aware of the needs that a child with ADHD has. It's not that these children are troublemakers like they've been made out to be, they simply need more time to understand concepts. Help influence the school system by sharing your experience with your child and sharing the tips that truly work with other parents.

## Keep Mindfulness in Mind

Much of the time, you and your family will need to remain patient and calm with your child. Their ADHD symptoms may start to become more manageable but ADHD is a lifelong condition and their inattention, struggle with sitting still, and forgetfulness may never fully disappear. For the rest of your life with your child, you will have to keep in mind that they may have difficulty listening, paying attention, and not "zoning out" in the middle of your conversation. Your child will, however, improve in a myriad of ways. Likely, your child will learn emotional control and be able to battle back the impulses to do things they shouldn't.

When you find yourself frustrated with them as they go through their academic lives, remain calm and don't forget to respond rather than react. Elementary and middle school can be particularly difficult as executive functioning may not have had enough time to be fostered adequately yet. However, "these skills are extremely malleable and amenable to improvement," says Johanna Calderon of Harvard Health (Calderon, 2020). This means that executive functioning in children can be boosted and developed at very early ages. Calderon goes on to suggest that the answer to much of the stress related to your child's ADHD-related executive functioning status is mindfulness: "To tackle both stress reduction and executive function improvement at once, mindfulness training seems like an ideal candidate" (2020). Try practicing mindfulness techniques you've learned in this book with your child and see how their listening skills are much more improved after the technique is over.

Remember the wings of mindfulness we discussed in the last chapter: wisdom and observation. Keep your mind open and watch as your child goes about their academic life, intervening with loving-kindness as they need. Children with ADHD may need more love and reassurance from their parents due to the difficulty they experience in school. The idea isn't to help them ace classes–although they might need assistance with this as well–but instead to make sure they understand that it's okay if they aren't fully understanding everything.

## EXERCISE: Mindfully Moving

Try this exercise with your child and see how they respond to the technique. This can help your child–who may have trouble with constant distraction–draw back into the present moment without interruption.

First, begin walking. Then, when you are at a comfortable pace (ideally, a slow pace in an environment that brings you and your child comfort and peace), begin saying "left, right" with each movement of the corresponding leg movement. This means you'll say "left" when your left foot goes forward and "right" when your right foot goes forward. Continue this technique for just a few minutes and observe how being in the present moment affects your child's mood, listening skills, and peace of mind.

While this may feel boring at first, the idea is to bring your child's mind to the current moment and free them of any other thoughts so they can practice their attention skills.

## Action Plan: Assist With Your Child's Academic Success

First and foremost, your plan of action for academics with your child is to remember to keep your cool and be mindful. Mindfully think about your child's educational progress and keep yourself in a state of calm. Your child may require more time and attention than other children, may need more help at home with their assignments, and may need more materials or assistance with projects. There's nothing wrong with this, although it can be frustrating when your forgetful child doesn't mention that their model of a cell is due at 9 am the following morning and you've already changed into pajamas, but now you must run to the store.

With time and patience, your mindful parenting skills will foster a healthy and safe connection for you and your child to tackle any academic challenges that may arise. Remember to use all the mindfulness techniques outlined in this book, especially the Mindfully Moving technique, wherein you forgo all other worries and remain as calm as possible while simply focusing on your movements. By doing so, you can release some of the frustration and worry that you may feel about your child's academic performance.

# ADHD Medication Options

*Medication*. The word itself can sound scary. Any parent in their right mind would blanch at the word and think, "Why does my child have to be on medication?" Concern and uncertainty about ADHD medication are normal. Truthfully, your child may not require medication. Ken Ensroth, a medical doctor and psychiatrist for Providence Child and Adolescent Psychiatry, discusses medication treatments for children with ADHD and their side effects. In this chapter, we will discuss his findings; however, he mentions: "Medication can never be a substitute for parental involvement. My best advice is to keep the lines of communication open with [your child], [their] teachers, and other people who are important in [their] life" (n.d.). No matter whether or not your family chooses to use medication for your child's ADHD symptoms, parental patience, love, and attention must always be present.

## Medication Facts and Myths

There are a lot of myths about ADHD medication that tend to get circulated and scare worried parents. Some of these myths have zero basis in reality. Here are a few that have been easily expelled by a 2019 blog post from Millenium Medical Associates:

- **Myth #1: ADHD medications are new and untested.** ADHD medications have actually been prescribed without long-term health effects for over 50 years.

- **Myth #2: ADHD medication is unsafe and has terrible side effects.** All medications have some side effects, yes, but the side effects of ADHD medications are not life-threatening or serious.

- **Myth #3: ADHD medications can act as gateway drugs.** Research actually suggests the opposite: ADHD patients who have been adequately treated are less likely to use illicit drugs.

- **Myth #4: You don't need to take your ADHD medication if you're not working or attending school.** Some people might be able to focus better at home than at school or work; for them, maybe this method works. It may not work for every patient. Each patient is advised to follow their doctor's regimen for medication and discuss with their doctor when it may be appropriate to skip a dose.

- **Myth #5: ADHD medication is unnecessary.** Everyone is different; some patients may not be able to function appropriately without ADHD medication. Focus for some ADHD patients can be so difficult and overwhelming that they do require medication.

## Pros and Cons of Medication

Most of the time, stimulants are used to help aid or erase the symptoms of ADHD, but they can have different effects on everyone. Sometimes, a doctor may have to try a few in order to find the one that works the best for your child. These stimulants work to "improve concentration, memory and organization by boosting the effectiveness of neurotransmitters, the chemical messengers that carry information throughout the brain" (Ensroth, n.d.). These stimulants typically take effect incredibly fast and patients are likely to see differences in a matter of days.

Benefits of ADHD medication include the following:

- Improved attention
- Decline in hyperactivity
- Reduction in impulsiveness
- Boosted academic performance

Side effects are present with nearly every type of pharmaceutical. The side effects of ADHD medication can include:

- Mild loss of appetite
- Difficulty sleeping
- Frustration or anxiousness

Note, however, that some patients never experience any side effects from their ADHD medication.

Ensroth also mentions that if families are too nervous about medication options, there are other options to consider (Ensroth, n.d.). These options include working with teachers to improve academic performance, teaching your child organizational skills by using planners or agendas, and putting your child in a physically demanding sports or music program, which can help with social interaction and be a good outlet for energy.

## EXERCISE: Mindfully Making Decisions

Now that you have learned a little more about medication options for your child's ADHD, it's time to use mindfulness to keep yourself calm while making decisions. Remember the wings of mindfulness that we discussed earlier in this book: wisdom and loving-kindness. Use observation with compassion to decide, mindfully, which option is best for your child.

First, you'll want to sit in a peaceful place. You may want to close your eyes or bird-watch in the park while attempting this exercise. Bring your awareness to your lungs and your breathing. Focus on inhaling, holding your breath for a moment, and feeling the way your breath exits your body. When you feel a sense of calm come over you, think about your child's ADHD symptoms. Simply observe them in your head, remembering the times your child has struggled with forgetfulness, impulse control, or emotional regulation. Try to take your emotions out of the observations you're making in your head and simply accept and understand the behavior.

Next, consider how often your child's symptoms creep up. Are these symptoms a common disruptor in your child's daily life? How often are these symptoms interrupting your child's functioning? Consider if your child would benefit greatly from medication using only compassion as a lens. Think about how much you love your child and want what is best for them.

Some parents may decide that they would like to pursue medication to ease the discomfort their child may be feeling inside their busy minds while others may feel like their child can function at a typical range without medication. After using both wings of mindfulness, which side are you leaning towards?

Repeat this process as needed and discuss the choice with your partner as well. Show them how you thought about the choice to see if they have more insight to add to your situation.

## EXERCISE: Employing Loving-Kindness

Loving-kindness is a meditation that we have mentioned in this book a few times. Now, it's time to try it. This exercise is meant to give and receive love from yourself and from others.

First, you'll want to get in the most comfortable position possible. This can be seated, lying down, or however you'd like. Allow yourself to access a deep well of calm and open yourself up to the abstract concept of love. Imagine that you are sitting by a well and inside is a swirl of all the affection and love you hold. Now, you'll practice giving some of that affection you have for other people to yourself.

Ask yourself: What do I need? This may be hard for you to answer, and for some who are not used to caring for themselves, this can feel uncomfortable. Push the discomfort aside as much as you can and focus on the question, letting anything that comes into your mind take root. Perhaps you need more connection, love, or freedom. Whatever you need, write down or take a mental note.

Next, ask yourself: What do I most want to hear from other people? Feel free to write these down as well. Anything that makes you feel the most excited and giddy whenever someone says them to you, write them down and focus on how happy those words make you feel.

Now, you're going to give those words to yourself. For those who needed love or wanted to hear that they are loved, you'll say, "I love myself," or, "I love you," into a mirror. Other common chants or affirmations used during this process include:

- I am worthy of affection.
- May I know emotional peace from my strife.
- I belong.
- May I know that I am the architect of my life.
- I adore my ambition.

Try out any phrase that you think you need to hear and see how they feel. You may discover something about yourself was missing and you didn't even know.

## Action Plan: Make Treatment Decisions that Benefit Your Child

As your child's parent, you are the best person out there to decide what option is the best. Consider your child's quality of life in a mindful manner. Consider how they might benefit from ADHD medication. If they're an older child, ask them how they feel about the choice. If your child is younger, you may want to pursue cognitive behavioral therapy before using medication. With any option, there will be positives and negatives. The fact that you are even considering your options for your child's well-being means you are an amazing parent who loves their child and wants their success over everything else.

Bring awareness to yourself and your child and try to think about your options using the wings of mindfulness: compassion and observation. There are likely no wrong choices here.

# Conclusion

Mindfully parenting can be a difficult challenge, but the reward is rife with peace, patience, and a thriving relationship with your child. By adopting a mindful parenting approach to ADHD symptoms, you'll be helping your child focus on all the positives in life as opposed to catastrophizing all the negatives.

In this book, you've been armed with all the ADHD information needed to make the best possible decisions for your child's emotional, academic, and medical care. Perhaps, through these words, you have decided that therapeutic intervention would benefit your child, that you'd like to employ a reward system to help with difficult behaviors, or that you'd like to consult with your child's medical team to discuss medication options.

We've spent a great deal discussing research studies and information involving executive function and how incredibly important parental patience will be during a child's formative years, especially when they show symptoms of ADHD. It can be hard to keep your cool under the pressure of grocery store temper tantrums and emotional outbursts, but using the mindfulness techniques explored throughout these chapters, you now know how to best handle these situations. By stopping before reacting, bringing awareness to your breath, and taking fifteen slow breaths, you'll be ready to handle even the most difficult obstacles that arise from your beautiful child's ADHD symptoms.

One key factor to always remember is that you are incredibly important to your child; they rely on you for emotional support and mental fortitude. This is why your own self-care is so deeply necessary. Don't forget to pause and give yourself breaks as needed. Sometimes, you won't be able to keep going like a well-oiled machine.

Instead, you might need a small break to collect yourself before coming back to your child's needs. There's nothing wrong with scheduling some time to care for your own needs.

By making small changes to yourself, you'll be helping your family dynamic foster healthier communication and praise all of the good behaviors your child makes rather than making them feel bad for their misbehavior. With time and effort, you and your family are on your way to instilling a powerful mindful parenting approach that will keep you all functioning at your very best while keeping the lines of communication open for your child's needs.

You have been given so many tools throughout this book. Now, it's time for you to use them to support and nurture that beautiful child of yours.

# References

*Book Cover Image: Freepik.com. This cover has been designed using assets from Freepik.com*

*4 types of communication styles.* (2019, April 6). Alvernia University Online. Retrieved October 29, 2021, from https://online.alvernia.edu/articles/4-types-communication-styles/

Alidina, S. (2019, July 17). *Nine ways mindfulness reduces stress.* Mindful. Retrieved October 29, 2021, from https://www.mindful.org/9-ways-mindfulness-reduces-stress/

Anthony, M. (n.d.). *How to foster independence. Scholastic.* Retrieved October 29, 2021, from https://www.scholastic.com/parents/family-life/social-emotional-learning/social-skills-for-kids/how-to-foster-independence.html

Barkley, R. (2021, September 23). *What is an executive function? 7 deficits tied to ADHD. ADDitude.* Retrieved October 29, 2021, from https://www.additudemag.com/7-executive-function-deficits-linked-to-adhd/

Bertin, M. (2021, July 5). *The effects of ADHD on communication.* The A.D.D. Resource Center. Retrieved October 29, 2021, from https://www.addrc.org/effects-adhd-communication/

Bertin, M. (2020, November 17). *How everyday mindfulness can make you a better parent.* ADDitude. Retrieved October 29, 2021, from https://www.additudemag.com/mindful-parenting-adhd-managing-stress/

Bertin, M., Goldstein, E., Ellison, K., Rossy, L., Bullock, B. G., Whitney-Coulter, A., Naidoo,

U., & Smookler, E. (2018, October 15). *Mindful parenting for ADHD*. Mindful. Retrieved October 29, 2021, from https://www.mindful.org/mindful-parenting-for-adhd/

Bjarnadottir, A. (2019, June 19). *Mindful eating 101 - A beginner's guide*. Healthline. Retrieved October 29, 2021, from https://www.healthline.com/nutrition/mindful-eating-guide#tips

Calderon, J. (2020, December 16). *Executive function in children:* Why it matters and how to help. Harvard Health. Retrieved October 29, 2021, from https://www.health.harvard.edu/blog/executive-function-in-children-why-it-matters-and-how-to-help-2020121621583

Centers for Disease Control and Prevention. (2021, September 2). *School changes - helping children with ADHD*. Centers for Disease Control and Prevention. Retrieved October 29, 2021, from https://www.cdc.gov/ncbddd/adhd/features/adhd-and-school-changes.html

Davis, T. (n.d.). *Self-care: 12 ways to take better care of yourself*. Psychology Today. Retrieved October 29, 2021, from https://www.psychologytoday.com/us/blog/click-here-happiness/201812/self-care-12-ways-take-better-care-yourself

*Decluttering your mind and space with mindfulness*. (2020, March 11). eMindful. Retrieved October 29, 2021, from https://emindful.com/2020/03/11/decluttering-with-mindfulness/

*Diagnosing ADHD*. CHADD. (2020, October 6). CHADD. Retrieved October 29, 2021, from https://chadd.org/about-adhd/diagnosing-adhd/

*Emotional health is more important than grades*. (2020, October 12). Reach Out Recovery. Retrieved October 29, 2021, from https://reachoutrecovery.com/your-childs-mental-health-is-more-important-than-grades/

Ensroth, K. (n.d.). *Ask an expert: Should I put my child on ADHD medication?* Providence Health & Services, Oregon and Southwest Washington. Retrieved October 29, 2021, from https://oregon.providence.org/forms-and-information/a/ask-an-expert-should-i-put-my-child-on-adhd-medication/

*Evaluating childhood ADHD*. (2020, September 21). CHADD. Retrieved October 29, 2021, from https://chadd.org/for-parents/evaluating-for-childhood-adhd_qf/

*Focus more to ease stress*. (2011, December 6). Harvard Health. Retrieved October 29, 2021, from https://www.health.harvard.edu/healthbeat/focus-more-to-ease-stress

Goldstein, E. (2019, February 26). *Stressing out? S.T.O.P.* Mindful. Retrieved October 29, 2021, from https://www.mindful.org/stressing-out-stop/

Glowiak, M. (2020, April 14). *What is self-care and why is it important for you?* Southern New Hampshire University. Retrieved October 29, 2021, from https://www.snhu.edu/about-us/newsroom/health/what-is-self-care

Harpin, V. A. (2005, February 1). *The effect of ADHD on the life of an individual, their family, and community from preschool to adult life.* Archives of Disease in Childhood. Retrieved October 29, 2021, from https://adc.bmj.com/content/90/suppl_1/i2

Hasan, S. (Ed.). (2020, June). *Parenting a child with ADHD (for parents) - nemours kidshealth. KidsHealth.* Retrieved October 29, 2021, from https://kidshealth.org/en/parents/parenting-kid-adhd.html

*How to help your child with ADHD complete tasks.* (n.d.). Brain Balance Achievement Centers. Retrieved October 29, 2021, from https://www.brainbalancecenters.com/blog/how-to-help-your-child-with-adhd-complete-tasks

*How to succeed in high school with ADHD: A teen's guide.* (2021, July 29). ADDitude. Retrieved October 29, 2021, from https://www.additudemag.com/high-school-success-adhd-students-homework-studying/

Low, K. (2020, January 7). *How to set up a reward system for improving your child's ADHD behavior.* Verywell Mind. Retrieved October 29, 2021, from https://www.verywellmind.com/behavior-management-for-adhd-20867

Low, K. (2020, September 27). *What are the effects of impaired executive functions?* Verywell Mind. Retrieved October 29, 2021, from https://www.verywellmind.com/what-are-executive-functions-20463

Low, K. (n.d.). *Understand what it's like for children with ADHD.* Verywell Mind. Retrieved October 29, 2021, from https://www.verywellmind.com/understanding-children-with-adhd-20686#effects-of-adhd-in-kids

*Common misconceptions about ADHD medications.* (2019, March 11). Millennium Medical Associates - Adult ADHD Treatment in Los Angeles. Retrieved October 29, 2021, from https://www.millenniummedicalassociates.com/blog/2019/3/11/common-misconceptions-about-adhd-medications

*Mindful breathing.* (n.d.). Greater Good in Action. Retrieved October 29, 2021, from https://ggia.berkeley.edu/practice/mindful_breathing

*Mindful parenting: ADHD and Communication.* (2018, July 20). CHADD. Retrieved October 29, 2021, from https://chadd.org/attention-article/mindful-parenting-adhd-and-communication/

Morin, A. (2019, October 22). *How to know if you're a perfectionist parent and what to do about it.* Verywell Family. Retrieved October 29, 2021, from https://www.verywellfamily.com/what-to-know-about-perfectionist-parenting-4163102

Morin, A. (2021, July 2). *How cognitive reframing works.* Verywell Mind. Retrieved October 29, 2021, from https://www.verywellmind.com/reframing-defined-2610419

*Attention deficit hyperactivity disorder (ADHD).* (n.d.). NHS. Retrieved October 29, 2021, from https://www.nhs.uk/conditions/attention-deficit-hyperactivity-disorder-adhd/symptoms/

Orenstein, B. W. (n.d.). *Managing ADHD when routines change - ADHD and your child.* Everyday Health. Retrieved October 29, 2021, from https://www.everydayhealth.com/hs/adhd-and-your-child/managing-adhd-when-routines-change/

Pace, K. (2018, September 20). *Your mindfulness practice can be formal or informal.* MSU Extension. Retrieved October 29, 2021, from https://www.canr.msu.edu/news/your_mindfulness_practice_can_be_formal_or_informal

Rawe, J. (2021, January 28). *ADHD and the brain.* Understood. Retrieved October 29, 2021, from https://www.understood.org/articles/en/adhd-and-the-brain

Scaccia, A. (2020, August 26). *Depression and vitamin D deficiency.* Healthline. Retrieved October 29, 2021, from https://www.healthline.com/health/depression-and-vitamin-d

Selva, J. (2021, June 21). *History of mindfulness: From east to west and religion to science.* Positive Psychology. Retrieved October 29, 2021, from https://positivepsychology.com/history-of-mindfulness/

Storebø, O. J., Krogh, H. B., Ramstad, E., Moreira-Maia, C. R., Holmskov, M., Skoog, M., Nilausen, T. D., Magnusson, F. L., Zwi, M., Gillies, D., Rosendal, S., Groth, C., Rasmussen, K. B., Gauci, D., Kirubakaran, R., Forsbøl, B., Simonsen, E., & Gluud, C. (2015, November 25). *Methylphenidate for attention-deficit/hyperactivity disorder in children and adolescents: Cochrane systematic review with Meta-analyses and trial sequential analyses of randomised clinical trials.* The BMJ. Retrieved October 29, 2021, from https://www.bmj.com/content/351/bmj.h5203

*Studies link ADHD and communication problems.* (n.d.). Brain Balance Achievement Centers. Retrieved October 29, 2021, from https://www.brainbalancecenters.com/blog/adhd-and-communication-problems

Tuckman, A. (2021, September 6). *Why is an ADHD diagnosis so important?* ADDitude. Retrieved October 29, 2021, from https://www.additudemag.com/why-is-an-adhd-diagnosis-so-important/

Ricardo, C. (2019, October 24). *The two wings of the bird; mindfulness and self compassion.* A Caring Counselor. Retrieved October 29, 2021, from https://acaringcounselor.com/the-two-wings-of-the-bird-mindfulness-and-self-compassion/

*Large-scale MRI study confirms ADHD brain differences.* (2020, October 22). Understood. Retrieved October 29, 2021, from https://www.understood.org/articles/en/large-scale-mri-study-confirms-adhd-brain-differences?_sp=87ea7a1f-e259-4124-a609-cc90ede2d4cd.1634059451756

*Does ADHD raise the risk of mental health issues?* (2021, April 19). Understood. Retrieved October 29, 2021, from https://www.understood.org/articles/en/does-adhd-raise-risk-mental-health-issues

*Why you need to make time for self-care.* (n.d.). Retrieved October 29, 2021, from https://selecthealth.org/blog/2019/05/why-you-need-to-make-time-for-self-care

Wiener, J. (2020, September 4). *The ripple effect of ADHD in adolescents: Self-perceptions and social relationships.* SAGE Journals. Retrieved October 29, 2021, from https://journals.sagepub.com/doi/abs/10.1177/0829573520936456?journalCode=cjsa

Williams, P., & ADDitude Editors. (2021, May 27). *ADHD in children: Symptoms, evaluations & treatments.* ADDitude. Retrieved October 29, 2021, from https://www.additudemag.com/adhd-in-children-symptoms-diagnosis-treatment/

Williamson, J. (2021, February 16). *Self-talk when you can't control other people: 18 affirmations to keep you moving forward.* Healing Brave. Retrieved October 29, 2021, from https://healingbrave.com/blogs/all/self-talk-when-you-cant-control-other-people

*Your day is getting better - starting now.* (2021, March 24). ADDitude. Retrieved October 29, 2021, from https://www.additudemag.com/slideshows/adhd-famous-quotes-for-a-bad-day/

# ADHD Workbook for Kids (5-11)

70 Engaging Exercises to Encourage Mindful Meditation, Self-Reflection, and Improved Focus in Children with ADHD

Natalie Morgan

# Introduction

*"You're part of a very special club, and it's a gift. Do not let anyone tell you that you are not good enough."*
**- Orlando Bloom. Actor, ADHD, & Dyslexic**

## Welcome to my ADHD Workbook For Kids.

I have written this book to help children ages five through eleven (although it would be pertinent for all school aged children) develop amazing skills to help them focus and organize, strengthening skills you as parents have already taught them (or are currently teaching them).

If you are new to the world of ADHD, the terms "executive function," "mindfulness," and "communication pathways" may sound confusing or overwhelming. That is what I am here to help with. I'm here to explain a bit about ADHD, how it works with your child's brain, and give you some guidance with tips, tricks, and exercises.

Everything in this book is designed to help you help your child, and everything in this book has been proven to work with children, as well.

When a child has ADHD, but no one knows how to assist them, it can become increasingly frustrating—not just for your child but for you as a parent, as well. ADHD children can be scattered, have impulsive ideas (and then act upon them), forget things, be messy, and have big emotions. But they are also bright, funny, creative children who have interests and desire to try out everything they can, usually with a burst of gusto until they realize the subject is not for them.

There are times when the label ADHD may seem scary, but trust me, that is just a stereotype placed on these energetic bundles of excitement because before ADHD was researched, doctors didn't know what to do with them. Now, we have a ton of research, and the stigmas are falling away. Now, we can help our children become the best versions of themselves and have the happiest of lives.

## What is ADHD?

Attention Deficit Hyperactivity Disorder or ADHD is a neurodevelopmental disorder that can affect children and adults, causing impulsivity, disorganization, inattentiveness, and hyperactivity.[1] While it is normal for children to have problems focusing or staying still for long periods, children with ADHD will not grow out of the behaviors, which can worsen if they aren't taken care of, managed, or intervened in some way. Some symptoms of ADHD are:

- Excessive daydreaming
- Scattered behaviors where they forget or lose things
- Inability to sit still, to the point where they are always fidgeting
- Talking a lot
- Make careless mistakes and take unnecessary risks
- Cannot or will not resist temptation
- Dislike for waiting for their turn
- Socially awkwardness or failure to get along with others

As with everything, there are other factors and elements to take into consideration. Girls and boys may show these symptoms differently, and not all symptoms will show in all kids. My daughters both have different symptoms, and they are related.

While there is no understanding of what causes an ADHD brain to work the way it does, ADHD is manageable. In some cases, if maintained and trained consistently, by the time your child reaches adulthood, their ADHD symptoms could go away altogether.

There are days when you won't know what to expect from your child and other days when they will simply amaze you. The fact that never changes is how much you love and want to help them.

---

1. "What is ADHD?" Centers for Disease Control and Prevention.

With this workbook, you will begin your first step in helping your child learn ADHD management and maintenance. The exercises in this book will help teach you how to help your child, even through the bigger, angrier emotions that come with frustration and misunderstandings. Once you complete this book, there are parent and children resources to continue your mindful journey through executive function, communication skills, and so much more.

You and your child are rockstars. Learning how to guide them through this difficult time will not only give you a chance to get to know them uniquely but also give them the understanding and knowledge of how you support and love them no matter what.

## What is Executive Function?

Executive functions are a group of skills vital to learning how to live and manage everyday life.[2] There are three executive function areas: working memory, cognitive flexibility, and inhibitory control. These three areas manage emotions, help you pay attention, stay organized, start tasks, and keep track of what you are doing. When ADHD comes into play with executive functions, many skill sets needed to cultivate good habits become skewed mostly because of the brain's activity and how it works against ADHD neural pathways. This means that your ADHD child has to build these functions with consistency, creativity, and compassion for themselves.

When a child has issues with their working memory, they will be unable to retain information to be used at a later date. Cognitive flexibility allows your child to think in many shades of gray instead of just black and white. While inhibitory control allows your children to ignore distractions, resist temptation, and incorporate self-control when needed.

Some skills relate to executive function that quickly becomes vital parts of their learning, social, and home lives. When a child cannot block out distractions, resist temptation, or think in more than just one or two ways, their skill sets become an issue in every environment of their reality.

Children with ADHD will struggle with reflection, processing information, and emotional management. Executive function is something we all use each day of our lives. Finding the best way to build your ADHD child up is going to be a remarkable experience.

---

2. "Understanding Executive Functioning Issues in Your Child." Understood.org.

## How to Use this Workbook

This workbook is designed to help you and your child learn more about ADHD and guide you to some helpful tips, tricks, exercises, and fun activities. There is no need to push your child to do exercises if you are sensing that they feel frustrated or are having a bad day.

Learning how to manage and build good habits should be fun for everyone, and no one needs to feel extra or added pressure. The best thing you can do for your child is complete everything in this book by giving them the choices of how many to do in one day or for how long of a time they should work on it. It doesn't matter how quickly you get through the book. What matters is the commitment you both make toward completing it.

By the end of this workbook, you and your child should have fantastic guidelines on how to help them deal with their working memory, impulse control, and cognitive skills. They will also be aware of their emotions and how they should react (not that they always will), and how to be kind to themselves when they make mistakes.

The exercises and activities in this workbook focus on home life, school life, and social life. Building these skills within these three focuses will give your child a chance to develop the skills they need later in life.

The object of the workbook is to become more familiar with positive and negative traits associated with ADHD. Once you understand something, both you and your child will maintain it better, even during the rough patches.

I suggest reading the letters together and then explaining each section to your child. If your child can read, have them read some of the exercise instructions to you and ask them questions to see if they understand what they are supposed to do. Have them ask questions before starting the activity and check in on them frequently while doing it. It is good for them to know that you are around to help them with anything, even if the tasks seem easy. Remember, it might not be so easy for them.

Walk away from the book when either of you becomes too frustrated or emotional, and revisit the section that brought frustration another time.

Otherwise, have fun, learn things, and enjoy your time together. I look forward to sharing my knowledge with you!

# Hello from the World of ADHD

*A Letter to Parents and Kids*

## Hello parents,

When you hear the word ADHD, you may think of the buzzwords and stigma of ADHD. However, things have changed so much regarding how people interact, view, and practice ADHD tools that the world of attention deficit disorder is starting to have a positive outlook.

I'm not going to sugarcoat things. Having a child with ADHD can be frustrating, exhausting, and overwhelming at times. But, there are also moments of joy, wonder, and inspiration your child can bring to your life with everything they take an interest in and everything they can do. I am here to help you figure out how to get those moments in line, how to react when the moment gets rough, and how to reward the moments when things are going well.

This workbook has 70 exercises to help teach the child in your life how to build self-confidence and learn about the organization. They will also understand making the right choices with food, rules, and impulsive decisions. I have guidelines and activities to help them learn to be aware of their actions in social settings, at home, and at school. There is also an opportunity for your child to make decisions on (some) of their own actions. Having your child see that they can be independent and still make good choices can help them build confidence in themselves, making them want to keep performing in positive ways.

When your child does the workbook, they are welcome to do it alone. Still, they may also need your help to answer questions about instructions, guidance on what next step to take, reminders to keep going through the activity, and encouragement that they are doing a good job. **I set out with only a few things in mind for this workbook:**

1. For the student to learn about ADHD
2. For the student to have fun
3. For children ages 5 through 11 (broadly speaking), it should help with impulse control and other ADHD symptoms

It's a great idea to work on some activities together and a nice opportunity for a bonding experience. Your child is an amazing mixture of brilliant, creativity, and energy, and you are the team who gets to help them harness their power into a super one.

## Hello kids,

Your brain is special and unique to you, and you are amazing!

Guess what? Your brain learns differently than some of the other people in the world, but that's a great thing because being different means you have a special way to look at life. Not one person today will be anything like you are.

It's great that you are here and going to work through this book with us today. Inside are fun activities that will help you learn how to handle your biggest emotions, keep track of your favorite items, eat healthy food, work your body out, get your homework done in the shortest amount of time, give yourself a chance for rewards, and discover new games to have fun!

This workbook has 70 activities that will help you learn more about yourself, teach you how to make some good choices, and give you a chance to make some of your own decisions too.

The only thing that I'm asking is for you to finish the activities you start. That is the most important part because of how your brain works. I know that it can sometimes be hard, but this book will help you do the hard stuff even when it feels like you don't want to.

Make sure to ask the grown-up to help you with any questions that you have. Maybe they can work with you on some activities too, not because you need help, but just because it is fun!

# ADHD & Me

*A comprehensive understanding of what ADHD means for my parents and me*

ADHD is a short version of the term Attention Deficient, Hyperactivity Disorder. This long word simply means that your brain works differently than other people's. When you're bored, sometimes you have problems sitting still. If you are disorganized, you can have issues with finding things. When you tell stories, you talk in a lot of detail. And sometimes you have trouble not following the rules when something is exciting, taking turns, and a few more things. However, this also means that you will learn a lot of stuff, think many things are interesting, and be able to take on all types of cool things that seem entertaining to you.

If your brain works like this, know that you are not alone. At least three million people in the world also have brains that act as yours does, so there are many great ways that they have figured out how to make things easier, better, and focused for you.

This workbook is set out to give you some fun activities that will help you learn how to work well with ADHD, just like so many other people do.

**But first, why don't you answer a few of questions:**

1. Do you have trouble keeping your room clean?

2. Do you like to daydream about new or cool things?

3. Do you have a hard time sitting still?

4. Do you have a hard time remembering where you left something?

5. Do you feel like you have to walk around all the time?

If you answered yes to any of those, know that it's normal for anyone with ADHD to have trouble doing anything on the list. That's what your parents and I are going to help you with. In this section, you'll work on some fun games that will help you learn a little bit about how ADHD works in your brain, what it means for you, and how to find all your good parts too.

You should work on this book with a parent or with a grown-up nearby in case you have any questions. You should also read the instructions very carefully. You don't want to miss something and go back to start over. That is the opposite of what you are trying to do.

This workbook will help you build good habits and give yourself a chance to keep things in order, not get frustrated, and learn how to stay calm in all situations. In this first section, "ADHD & Me," you'll start to understand how ADHD makes your brain work with the activity "What is ADHD," then, you can do some fun true or false answers with "The Truth About ADHD" game, and then figure out what symptoms of ADHD you have. Finally, you'll learn about the good parts of having ADHD plus learn about some famous people who have ADHD and are successful because they figured out how to make their ADHD work for them, not against them.

I am excited to have you start on the activities and look forward to helping you get into a great groove. Let's get started!

## What is ADHD?

ADHD means that Attention Deficit Hyperactivity Disorder, while these words may sound scary, trust me, they are not. That big, long string of words means that your brain works differently from other people. But you are not alone. There are a lot of people whose brain works like yours does too, and what's really amazing is that there are a ton of ways that you can help your brain because there is a lot of information, and scientists, doctors, and researchers have done a lot of studying up on ADHD to this point.

While they don't know what makes your brain work differently, they have many ways to help you work to be the best you can be.

In this section, you get a chance to do a mix and match activity of words that describe ADHD, and then there is a true and false section where you can guess (or know!) what statements about ADHD are true and what ones are false. Other activities will have you thinking about your ADHD symptoms and looking at the bright side of ADHD too.

# 1. Mix & Match Activity

Think of ADHD as your superpower. The way your brain works gives you undeniable strength. You have a sense of humor, drive, passion, and thoughts unmatched by other people. Below is a list of amazing traits that come with ADHD. Draw a line connecting one word to another to see how many amazing parts of your mind you truly have.

| | |
|---|---|
| Drive | Setbacks |
| ADHD | Challenge |
| Push Past | Hyperfocus |
| Sparkling | Giving |
| Face | Sharing |
| Generous | Genius |
| Happy | Intelligence |
| Brain | Brilliant |
| Excited | Flair |
| Difference | Friendship |
| Strong Sense | Kindness |
| Willing | Personality |
| Spontaneous | Brave |
| Hilarious | Fairness |
| Seeing | Risk-taking |
| Affectionate | Impulsivity |
| Loving | Surprises |
| Conversation | Caring |
| Compassion | Skills |
| Passionate | Persistent |
| Creative | Outlook |
| Motivated | Problem Solving |
| Memory | Work on many things at once |

## 2. The Truth About ADHD

In this activity, you will learn the truths about ADHD and some things that are false, too. Sometimes there will be a person who maybe doesn't understand what ADHD is, and this activity will help you explain it better to them. For this activity, you will answer True or False for each statement. At the end of this exercise, you'll find a key to see how many statements you marked right!

| True | False | Statements |
|---|---|---|
| | F | ADHD isn't a medical condition. |
| | | Kids with ADHD just need to try harder. |
| | | People with ADHD will never learn how to focus. |
| | | All kids with ADHD are hyperactive. |
| | | Only boys have ADHD. |
| | | ADHD is a learning disability. |
| | | Kids will outgrow ADHD. |
| | | ADHD is my parent's fault. |
| | | ADHD is not a serious condition. |
| | | ADHD is caused by sugar, food additives, or food allergies. |
| | | Kids who CAN focus well don't have ADHD. |
| | | ADHD symptoms can be improved by healthy eating and exercise. |
| | | You only have ADHD if you cannot focus. |
| | | Kids with ADHD have problems with timing and organization. |
| | | Kids with ADHD have an amazing way of looking at the world. |
| | | Anyone with ADHD works very hard, and they are very determined. |
| | | ADHD uses hyperfocus as a superpower. |
| | | People with ADHD aren't smart. |

|  |  | Sugar and processed foods can enhance ADHD symptoms. |
|---|---|---|
|  |  | Trying new things helps ADHD kids focus. |

## Answers:

**1.** *ADHD isn't a medical condition.* **FALSE.**

The American Psychiatric Association, the Center for Disease Control and Preventions, and The National Institutes of Health all name ADHD as a medical condition. ADHD is a common condition in children. The United States has millions of adults and kids who have ADHD.[3]

**6.** *Kids with ADHD just need to try harder.* **FALSE.**

Anyone who has ADHDparent'sady trying harder than other people. Because you find it harder to pay attention, you put forth more energy on paying attention.[4]

**7.** *People with ADHD will never learn how to focus.* **FALSE.**

By training your brain through exercise, eating, and routine-based activities, you are going to be able to focus better than you ever thought you could!

**8.** *All kids with ADHD are hyperactive.* **FALSE.**

Even though the word "hyperactive" is in the title, not all kids with ADHD have hyperactivity as a symptom. It just means that their brain goes in many directions simultaneously, which makes it hard to focus. If a child has hyperactivity as an adult, the symptom can lessen as they get older.[5]

**9.** *Only boys have ADHD.* **FALSE.**

While boys are two times as likely to be diagnosed with ADHD, girls have ADHD, too. It just looks different for girls than it does for boys, which is why it often goes unnoticed.[6]

**10.** *ADHD is a learning disability.* **FALSE.**

While ADHD can affect the way you learn, it isn't a learning disability. The

---

3. Morin, Amanda. "8 Common Myths About ADHD."
4. ibid.
5. Morin, Amanda. "8 Common Myths About ADHD."
6. ibid.

difference is how your brain works. A learning disability makes it harder to learn specific skills like reading or math. Kids with ADHD have trouble with global skills, which means they have trouble controlling impulsive thoughts and have difficulty paying attention. These skills can make it tough to do well in any subject.[7]

11. *Kids will outgrow ADHD.* **FALSE.**

    While symptoms can lessen over the years, ADHD never truly goes away. However, you can train your brain to focus and organize so you can function in the best way possible.[8]

12. *ADHD is my parent's fault.* **FALSE.**

    ADHD can be helped with parents' support, but it is not your parent's fault. You were born with a different way of seeing the world. If someone says something about your parents, know that this person or people does not understand the way ADHD works. ADHD is a medical condition and has nothing to do with how your parents treat or respond to you.

13. *ADHD is not a serious condition.* **FALSE.**

    Yes, it is. The Center for Disease Control (CDC) states that "ADHD can cause problems in how well children do in school, their ability to make and keep friends, and how they function in society. Although there are treatments to improve ADHD symptoms, more information is needed about managing ADHD so children can learn, and grow, into adulthood without being impaired by their symptoms."[9]

14. *ADHD is caused by sugar, food additives, or food allergies.* **FALSE.**

    While brain function can be affected by the food children eat, no one develops ADHD overnight. ADHD is an obstacle that all people are born with.

15. *Kids who CAN focus well don't have ADHD.* **FALSE.**

    ADHD affects every person differently. Even twins who have ADHD issues can have different symptoms.

16. *ADHD symptoms can be improved by healthy eating and exercise.* **TRUE!**

---

7. "Is ADHD a Learning Disability?" Medical News Today.
8. Morin, Amanda. "8 Common Myths About ADHD."
9. "Research on ADHD." Centers for Disease Control and Prevention.

Have you ever heard, "You are what you eat?" That is a true statement. Putting healthy, organic, and whole foods into your body makes it work better. Plus, when you exercise, like running or playing basketball, you will burn off some of the energy that ADHD gives you with little effort.

17. *You only have ADHD if you cannot focus.* **FALSE.**

    While ADHD makes it harder for you to focus, once you figure out the best way to organize yourself and get into a nice routine, you will be able to focus and do your best a lot!

18. *Kids with ADHD have problems with timing and organization.* **True and False.**

    Before someone told you that you have ADHD, you probably had a hard time keeping things clean. But, once you work with a routine and understand more about ADHD, you can be more organized than others because the organization and routine help your brain work really, really well.

19. *Kids with ADHD have an amazing way of looking at the world.* **TRUE!**

    Because of the way your mind works, you will be able to look at the world from a view that no one else can see. Only you will be able to come up with special answers to the same problems that everyone else has. It's going to be great.

20. *Anyone with ADHD works very hard, and they are very determined.* **TRUE!**

    Even though you do things like everyone else, you work harder to find the right way that works for you. This process makes you work harder and longer, and it gives you a reason to come up with the best plan for how your brain works best.

21. ADHD uses hyperfocus as a superpower. **TRUE!**

    When you are interested in a specific topic or trying to solve a complex problem, your ability to focus until you finish or come up with an answer is amazing. Your hyperfocus is truly your superpower!

22. People with ADHD are very intelligent. **TRUE!**

    Because your brain works the way it does, it means that your thoughts and mind work faster than some people without ADHD. This means that you can have double the amount of ideas that another person has in the same amount of time. Sounds pretty smart to me!

23. Sugar and processed foods can enhance ADHD symptoms. **TRUE!**

    Again, think about how you eat and what goes into your body. If you put good food in, your body can do things well. If you put bad food into your body, it will start to work badly. The problem is that sometimes food that is bad for you tastes very good, but the only reason it tastes so good is that there are so many bad ingredients. You'll want to be cautious about eating them and talk with your parents about the right way to eat good food.

24. Trying new things helps ADHD kids focus. **TRUE!**

    One of the most fantastic things about having ADHD is that you are interested in trying out a LOT of different activities. The bonus part of your interest in so many items is that you burn away your extra ADHD energy and learn more about topics you didn't before. Trying new things will help you focus on every part of your life because you are using your energy in a great way!

## 3. What Are ADHD Symptoms, and What Symptoms Do I Have?

Although there are very specific symptoms, ADHD affects everyone differently. Not everyone has the same symptoms, so here is an activity about ADHD symptoms and what can happen when you can't manage ADHD. Circle the symptoms that seem like you have and read the consequences if you don't find a way to work with it, but what can happen when you solve your ADHD symptom puzzle.

### Unable to Focus

*Consequences*

- Does not pay attention to homework details
- Makes careless mistakes on class assignments
- Cannot keep your attention when playing
- Cannot keep attention when doing other tasks like chores, homework, etc.
- Does not seem to listen when being spoken to

- Forgets to follow through on instructions
- Will not follow through after starting chores, homework, or other tasks
- Has a problem organizing homework, room, activities, and other tasks
- Avoid anything you dislike
- Avoid anything that needs to have sustained brainpower (especially homework)
- Becomes distracted easily
- Can lose toys, pencils, books, assignments, and more
- Forgets daily activities

*Rewards When You Solve the Focus Puzzle*

- Able to multitask
- Able to hyperfocus
- Able to organize everything and know where everything is
- Will not miss homework assignments
- Will learn to pay attention to your instructions and details
- Will begin to learn how to listen better
- Will try new things
- Will be able to focus even when you start to get distracted
- Keep your toys, pencils, books, etc., in one place and won't lose much anymore

## **Hyperactivity**

*Consequences*

- Moves a lot, cannot sit still
- Does not like to sit in a seat
- Leaves their place without warning
- Leaves their seat in unsuitable situations

- Unable to play quietly
- Unable to work quietly
- Always "going"
- Talks quickly in bursts
- Talks a lot

**Rewards When You Solve the Hyperactivity Puzzle**

- Can get a lot done in a short amount of time
- Can try new activities that interest them while still doing other activities
- Can stand or sit in one place when you are expected to
- Can learn to sit still
- Learns how to work while still moving
- Learns how to work while being noisy
- Can use their talking skills for debate, theater, cheerleading, and other activities

## Impulsivity

*Consequences*

- Answers a question before the full question is asked
- Does not like to and cannot wait their turn
- Interrupts conversations
- Butts into other people talking
- Will do unsafe things in unsafe situations
- Will not think before speaking, doing, or acting
- May do something they aren't supposed to do because they cannot wait

**Rewards When You Solve the Impulsivity Puzzle**

- Waits to hear the whole question

- Waits for their turn

- Listens to other people when they are talking

- Thinks before they act

- Will think of consequences of unsafe situations

- Will use impulsivity for spontaneous

## 4. The Sunny Side of ADHD

Even though it takes a little bit of time to find the right balance to make you be your best self with ADHD, there are a lot of amazing traits that come along with it. Go through this activity with a grownup to find some things that interest you. You can try out these things and find people who have used their ADHD to become successful in life.

| | | |
|---|---|---|
| Ice Skating | Fishing | Puzzles |
| Reading | Video Games | Tennis |
| Pickle Ball | Basketball | Baseball |
| Cheerleading | Painting | Writing |
| Reading | Parkour | Softball |
| Tag football | Touch football | Football |
| Cooking | Baking | Drawing |
| Board Games | Movie Making | Photography |
| Singing | Guitar | Drums |
| Flute | Piano | Saxophone |
| Musical Instruments | Chess | Knitting |
| Ride a Skateboard | Sewing | Fashion Design |
| Jewelry Design | Coloring books | Soccer |
| Debating | Theater | Meditating |
| Science Experiments | Looking at the Stars | Having a picnic |
| Learning about Stars | Learning about Dinosaurs | Learning about Science |
| STEM Topics | Learn about Bugs | Learn about Animals |
| Do Some Mazes | Play Games | Do Chores for Money |
| Play Hockey | Swimming | Build a Robot |
| Invent Something New | Take an Electronic Apart | Build with Legos or Blocks |

| Put on a Play | Make a Puppet | Camp Inside |
| Camp Outside | Build Something with Tools | Ride a Bike |

## 5. ADHD Success Stories

When you mix your energy and what you love together, you can live your life in the way you want to. Look through this list of successful and famous people to see what could interest you. Also, know that they have ADHD just like you! If you don't know them why not try researching them on the internet and finding out more about them.

| Simone Biles | Olympic Gymnast, medal winner, activist |
|---|---|
| Lisa Ling | Award-winning journalist and TV personality[10] |
| Will Smith | Singer, Song-writer, Actor, Producer, Director |
| will.i.am | Singer, song-writer, performer, actor, producer, fashion designer |
| Michael Phelps | Olympic medalist for swimming[11] |
| Dusty Davis | Professional NASCAR Racer |
| Scott Kelly | Astronaut |
| Solange Knowles | Singer, song-writer, actor |
| Channing Tatum | Actor, dancer, director, producer |
| Michelle Carter | Olympic medalist in shot put |
| Adam Levine | Singer, song-writer |
| Justin Timberlake | Singer, song-writer, actor, producer |
| David Flink | Activist[12] |

---

10. "Celebrity Spotlight: Why Journalist Lisa Ling Was 'Relieved' by Her ADHD Diagnosis." Understood.com.
11. "Celebrity Spotlight: How Michael Phelps' ADHD Helped Him Make Olympic History." Understood.com.
12. "Video: Activist David Flink on Growing up with ADHD and Dyslexia." Understood.com.

As you can see, the people above took many different directions. You have a singer, a racecar driver, a dancer, a writer, athletes, and more. Never let yourself believe that just because you have ADHD that you can achieve what you want. It is the opposite. You can reach your dreams and go further because of your driven and creative nature.

# I Am Stronger than ADHD

*A guide to every day coping skills*

Just because you have ADHD doesn't mean there is anything bad going on inside your head. It's just the opposite. Now that you know how your brain works, you can understand how your mind works in a better way. This information will help you figure out how to separate yourself from ADHD and teach you how to make better choices, how to study your best, and how to be more organized. We have some activities below to help.

## 6. What Does ADHD Look Like?

When you think of ADHD, what do you think about? Does ADHD look like a spinning top? A puppy? Does it feel like you are swinging on a swing and are going very high? Does ADHD look like you are eating a lot of cookies? Think about what ADHD looks like to you and draw it on the sheet below. Think about this image every time you start to get overwhelmed, feel frustrated, or want to do something that might be dangerous. You are creative and smart, and when you have an ADHD moment, if you picture this image, it will help give your ADHD a shape, it will help make ADHD more real for you.

## 7. What Do YOU Look Like?

Now, draw a picture of you. You can make this picture of you doing anything you'd like.

## 8. What Do YOU Look Like with ADHD?

Now, think about what you look like with ADHD. Are you happy? Do you see yourself as an astronaut or a singer one day in the future? Where is the ADHD? Is it helping you make your future bright? Are you guiding and managing your ADHD with the help of your parents or a grownup in your life? Is your room clean and your homework complete? It can be anything you want!

## 9. Your Vision Collage

For this activity, you are going to look through images of other people. Add photos of people doing something you find interesting or people you want to meet. Draw whatever you may wish, and put all of the photos on the same board.

When you make a collage, you will combine many different images and ideas that seem interesting to you. These ideas can be of who you want to be for your future self or something you really want to do, like go skiing or make the basketball team. Whatever you want for yourself, add an image to the collage.

**Step-by-Step Instructions:**

1. Get your supplies ready:
   - Posterboard
   - Glue or glue stick
   - 1 pair adult scissors, 1 pair safety scissors
   - Images printed from the internet.
   - Old magazines

2. Get images:

   - Old Magazines

     i. If you have old magazines, go through them with a grownup to find pictures that you like. These pictures can be images of people doing something that seems cool or good to you.

     ii. Rip or cut out the images and place them in a pile.

   - Online Pictures

     iii. If you don't have old magazines, you can look online with your grownup by typing in specific words like "fun activities," or "interesting people," "pets," "jobs," "food," and more.

     iv. Have a grownup print out the images and cut them, so the white border isn't showing anymore.

     v. Put these images in a pile.

3. Once you have all your images cut out and put in a pile, use a glue stick on the back of your image.

4. Flip the image over and lay it on an unused part of the poster board.

5. NOTE: Some images will overlap, meaning that some images may cover up a little part of another image. This overlap is okay! Just make sure not to cover the entire image up with another one.

6. Once you have glued all your images to the poster board, you can put your vision collage up in your room or the area in which you hang out the most. Then, every time you look at it, you can be reminded of what you want to do, which will help keep you focused!

# 10. What Does Organization Look Like to You?

Think about the word "organized." What does it mean to you? The definition of the word "organized" is "arranged in a specific way so that things can be found easily." An example of this is putting all your homework sheets into a special folder that is only used for homework.

Being organized helps you get ready on time and allows you to be able to find things when they are needed. Organization also gives you a chance for your mind to be calmer because you aren't living in a messy place.

Think about some items or tools that can help keep you organized. Draw them in the boxes below. Some examples of tools and items that can help you are a desk, book light, toy box, folders, shelves for homework papers, cups for your crayons, pencils, etc.

After you draw out your organizational tools, ask a grownup to help you get your room and play spaces organized with the items on your list.

If you could have rewards for good behavior, what would they be? Would you ask for books? Stickers? A slice of pizza? A donut? Draw some items below that you'd like to stick in a reward box, and have your grownup draw some items, too. Then, build a reward box together.

## How to Build a Reward Box

1. Go to a local craft store or your local "everything" store and look for a plain box. The box can be any size, but smaller boxes are good to start with. Smaller packages will look like they are quicker to fill, plus bigger rewards (like a pizza night) won't need to go into the box. Instead, you can write "pizza night" on a piece of paper.

2. Once you have your box, you can decorate it together! Add glitter, stickers, markings, paint, scrapbook paper, comic books, or anything to make the box fun, decorative, and exciting.

3. When you are done decorating the box, place it in a common area where your child will be able to see it daily as a reminder that the rewards are still there.

4. Go to a dollar store and stock up on stickers, small trinkets, sugar-free candies, and more. Anything to get you excited. Take the images you've drawn below and try to get as close to the drawings as you can.

5. If you have larger items that won't fit in your box, get some scrap paper or decorative scrapbook paper. Write the bigger rewards on little pieces of the designed paper, and then you can pull out some reward ideas when you need them.

## 12. You Are Stronger than ADHD

Make a list of positive words and how ADHD helps you be a stronger person. Add some words about how great your personality is, too!

| Smart | Funny | Bold |
|---|---|---|
| | | |
| | | |
| | | |
| | | |
| | | |
| | | |
| | | |
| | | |
| | | |
| | | |
| | | |
| | | |
| | | |
| | | |
| | | |
| | | |
| | | |
| | | |

When you are done filling out the good words about yourself, make sure to read them out with a grownup, like your mom, dad, aunt, uncle, grandma, grandpa, or someone else.

## 13. It's Time for Big Feelings

When you have ADHD, sometimes you have very big feelings. Sometimes, you can get EXTRA HAPPY, and other times you can get EXTRA ANGRY. When you are feeling anything EXTRA and it's making you feel jittery or like you want to yell out, then come to this book, draw your feelings, and read the helpful tips to see how you can work with your emotions in a healthy way.

### HAPPY

When you are feeling so happy you feel as though you are going to jump out of your skin, try:

**BUILD HEALTHY HABITS**

- ☐ Going for a walk
- ☐ Playing a sport
- ☐ Running around the block with a grown up
- ☐ Painting with bright colors
- ☐ _____
- ☐ _____
- ☐ _____
- ☐ _____

### ANGRY

When you are feeling so angry that you just want to break something, instead try:

**BUILD HEALTHY HABITS**

- ☐ Going for a walk or run
- ☐ Screaming into a pillow
- ☐ Squeezing a stress ball
- ☐ _____
- ☐ _____
- ☐ _____
- ☐ _____

## BRAVE

When you are feeling so brave that you think you can do anything right now, STOP and think about doing these things instead:

**BUILD HEALTHY HABITS**

- ☐ Write down 10 consequences of what you want to do
- ☐ Ask a parent their thoughts about your idea
- ☐ _____
- ☐ _____
- ☐ _____
- ☐ _____

## PROUD

When you have pride in something you are doing, you will feel happy about something you've done or a task you have finished:

**BUILD HEALTHY HABITS**

- ☐ Talk about your pride.
- ☐ Look at your work and think about how hard it was to finish what you were doing or what you did.
- ☐ _____
- ☐ _____
- ☐ _____
- ☐ _____

## CALM

A good feeling to have! When you feel relaxed you can sit still and have a quiet mind. With ADHD, there are times when you need to feel relief but don't know how. Come up with a list:

**BUILD HEALTHY HABITS**

- ☐ Take a bath
- ☐ Sit in a quiet room
- ☐ Listen to calm music
- ☐ _____
- ☐ _____
- ☐ _____
- ☐ _____

## WORRIED

Worry is when you are feeling scared about one thing. You think that something bad could happen but aren't sure:

**BUILD HEALTHY HABITS**

- ☐ Jump rope
- ☐ Clean your room
- ☐ Make a list
- ☐ Go play a sport
- ☐ _____
- ☐ _____
- ☐ _____
- ☐ _____

## STRESSED

When you feel stressed out, it can be hard to breathe, or you may feel tightness in certain parts of your body. People feel stressed when they have too much going on or are worried about trying something new:

**BUILD HEALTHY HABITS**

- ☐ Dance
- ☐ Write about it
- ☐ Take a bath
- ☐ _____
- ☐ _____
- ☐ _____
- ☐ _____

## TIRED

Being tired has an easy fix: usually, you can just go to sleep. But sometimes you cannot because you have to go to school, have to do chores, or have something important. Being tired can sometimes make you cranky, so come up with some healthy habits!

**BUILD HEALTHY HABITS**

- ☐ When you are tired, you can:
- ☐ Try running in place
- ☐ Drink some water
- ☐ Eat a banana
- ☐ _____
- ☐ _____
- ☐ _____
- ☐ _____

## FRUSTRATED

Being frustrated is hard! It means that you haven't gotten your way, something isn't working out the way it's supposed to, or someone isn't listening to you. There are ways to unwind your frustration, though, and you'll have to come up with some, too:

**BUILD HEALTHY HABITS**

- ☐ Take five deep breaths
- ☐ Count backwards from 10
- ☐ Draw a picture of your frustration
- ☐ _____
- ☐ _____
- ☐ _____
- ☐ _____

## ANNOYED

Sometimes things are so annoying that you just want to stomp your feet, yell, throw things, or give up.
Instead, try to create a list and build healthy habits:

**BUILD HEALTHY HABITS**

- ☐ Step away from the task that is annoying you
- ☐ Do a yoga pose
- ☐ _____
- ☐ _____
- ☐ _____
- ☐ _____

## FEAR

Being scared comes from new things, dark things, or something that made you jump. Fear is a small emotion that feels very big. But the great thing about this emotion is that once you overcome it, you can overcome anything:

**BUILD HEALTHY HABITS**

- ☐ Talking to a grownup
- ☐ Writing about your fear
- ☐ Drawing what you are afraid of
- ☐ _____
- ☐ _____
- ☐ _____
- ☐ _____

## SADNESS

Sadness can be a hard emotion to feel. When you have healthy habits, you can feel sad while still doing things, and that is a good practice to get into:

**BUILD HEALTHY HABITS**

☐ Write about your sadness
☐ Take a nap
☐ Watch a movie
☐ Wrap yourself up in a blanket
☐ _____
☐ _____
☐ _____
☐ _____

## CONFUSED

When you feel confused, sometimes you can start to get angry, frustrated, uncomfortable, or sad. You can also start to say mean things about yourself, which is never a good thing. Try the healthy habit tips here and help build your ideas, too:

**BUILD HEALTHY HABITS**

☐ Ask a parent to help explain
☐ Take a deep breath
☐ Try to figure out what you are confused about and why you have confusion
☐ Say three nice things about yourself
☐ _____
☐ _____
☐ _____
☐ _____

## UNCOMFORTABLE

When you are comfortable, you are relaxed, warm, and usually in a familiar place. Uncomfortable is the opposite of this. Usually, discomfort happens when you are in a new place or when someone points out that you don't know something. Don't worry when this happens. We all have been there:

Brainstorm!

### BUILD HEALTHY HABITS

- ☐ Hold someone's hand
- ☐ Talk about your feelings
- ☐ Keeps a stuffed animal with you
- ☐ _____
- ☐ _____
- ☐ _____
- ☐ _____

## 14. Distractions, Distractions, Everywhere!

Distractions are everywhere you look when you have ADHD. It can be something as simple as looking at the pattern in a bag of onions or something bigger like the interruption of a fire truck siren during a test. Once you become distracted, it's hard to pull your mind back to the original project, task, or class in front of you.

This activity will have you list out a bunch of distractions and come up with some helpful tips that will direct you back to your original task. On the first line, write an example of the distraction. On the second line, add a helpful tip that will redirect you away from the distraction and help you focus on the initial activity.

Distraction: _____

Tip: Pick the toy up and give it to your parents. You can play with it as a reward once your homework is done.

Distraction: _____

Tip: _____

Distraction: _____

Tip: _____

Distraction: _____

Tip: _____

Distraction:

Tip:

Distraction:

Tip:

Distraction:

Tip:

Distraction:

Tip:

Distraction:

Tip:

## 15. Treasure Trove

This activity is fun for the whole family. Have a child and grownup collect interesting things or "treasures" from around the house. Then, have the grownup hide them in a few treasure boxes. The grownup can make a quick map of where the child has to find them. Include instructions on the map that the child has to follow, like "take one BIG step over the broom on the floor," or "crawl up the stairs, carefully." Using instructions like these activate the child's ability to pay attention to instructions and continue to focus at the same time. After the child gets used to the easy maps, you can create more challenging maps with different types of treasures.

# How to Make Good Choices

*Dealing with Emotions, Impulses, and Listening Skills*

There will be times when your ADHD takes over, making it hard to deal with your emotions, control your impulsive ideas, and listen to what is going on around you. When you aren't paying attention, you could get hurt, miss an instruction, or receive a consequence that you don't want. Try these activities below to understand what could happen if you act on an impulsive thought and the things you can miss if you aren't paying attention.

## 16. Stop. Think!

This activity works with impulsivity. When you have ADHD, you have a lot of ideas! Your ideas are creative and interesting, just like you. But sometimes, the ideas you have may not be safe or healthy to carry out in real life, and your ADHD mind may tell you to do it RIGHT NOW. This activity will help kids learn to stop and think about the consequences of their actions.

Before you do it, stop and think about the consequences of your actions.

| EXAMPLE | STOP. THINK! | QUESTIONS TO ASK YOURSELF |
|---|---|---|
| You are bored and no longer want to do homework. You decide cutting your hair is a better idea. |  | Do I really want my hair cut?<br>Does my hair need to be cut right now?<br>Isn't my homework more important?<br>Should I take a break before I do anything else? |
| You walk into the kitchen, and no one is around. You see a chocolate pie sitting there. Suddenly, you realize how hungry you are. |  | Who is the pie for?<br>Is eating pie really healthy for me?<br>Am I really hungry?<br>What will happen if I eat it? |
| No one is home, and you aren't sure what to do with yourself. You've done your homework, and you've used your video game time up. But if no one is home to know you're playing, is it that bad of an idea? |  | Should I play the video game?<br>What harm could come if I play the game?<br>Am I breaking the rules? |
| You are in school and you see that your friend is making something on his desk. You can't see what it is, so you start to lean back in your chair. |  | What could happen here?<br>Can you ask your friend later what they were making?<br>Are you going to get hurt?<br>How important is finding out? |

The teacher has been talking for a while. She is explaining something about how to take care of an assignment or task, but your mind is starting to wander. Instead of listening, you start drawing a scene between aliens and sea creatures. Then a worksheet gets placed in front of you, but you don't know what to do.

Think about your choices.

What can you do with the worksheet?

What can you do with your story?

What can you do to reset yourself?

You are pretty upset. One person you thought was your friend decided to invite someone else over to their house instead of you. You are so angry you could throw something, and you want to rip things off of the wall.

How will ripping something off of the wall help you feel better?

How will throwing something make you feel better?

Would it be better to speak to someone about how angry you are?

You are very excited. You've just gotten added to the team at school. You cannot wait to begin practice, but it is raining outside. So, you decide that the living room is almost as big as a basketball court. The idea of playing is so great. You start a game of you and no one else, then you jump and shoot the ball.

Are you supposed to have a ball in the house?

Are you thinking about what happens if you break something?

Is it time to put the ball somewhere you cannot see it, so you don't get tempted to use it?

Your dad is busy at home, and your mom is still at work. You want some brownies and decide that you want to make them. You don't know how, but you think you can wing it since your dad is busy. Halfway through the process, you look into the living room and realize the TV is on.

What would your dad say?

Do you have permission to use the stove?

Does your mom want to come home from work to a big mess in the kitchen?

How badly do you want brownies?

Isn't there something else you could do while you wait for a grownup's help?

Now, come up with some real-life examples of when you didn't listen, acted impulsively, or had some big emotions. If you had STOPPED and THOUGHT, what would the questions have been to make things better?

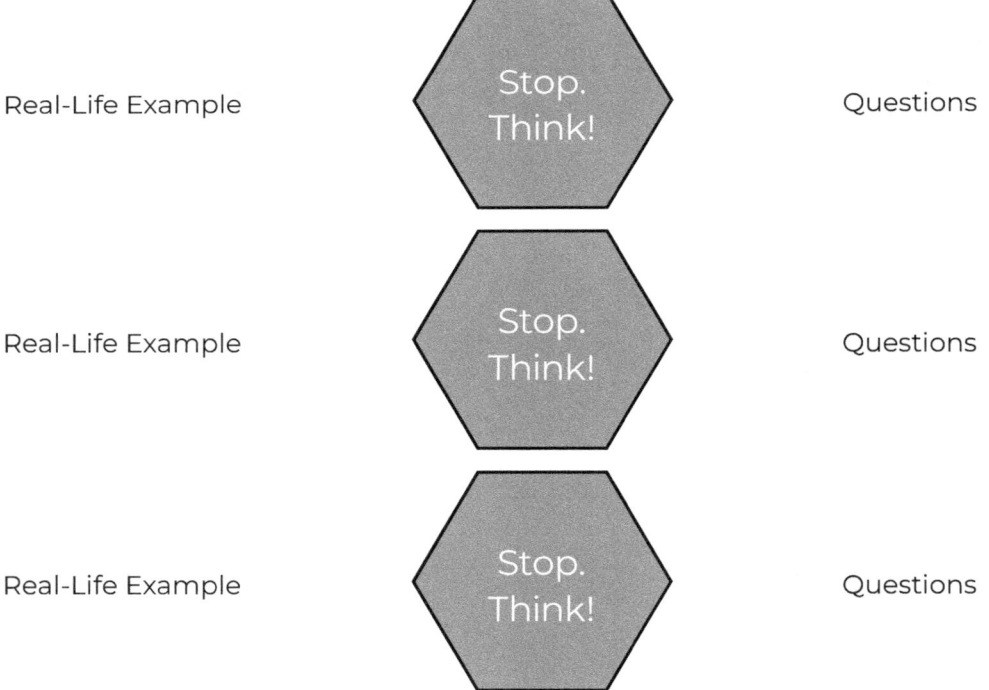

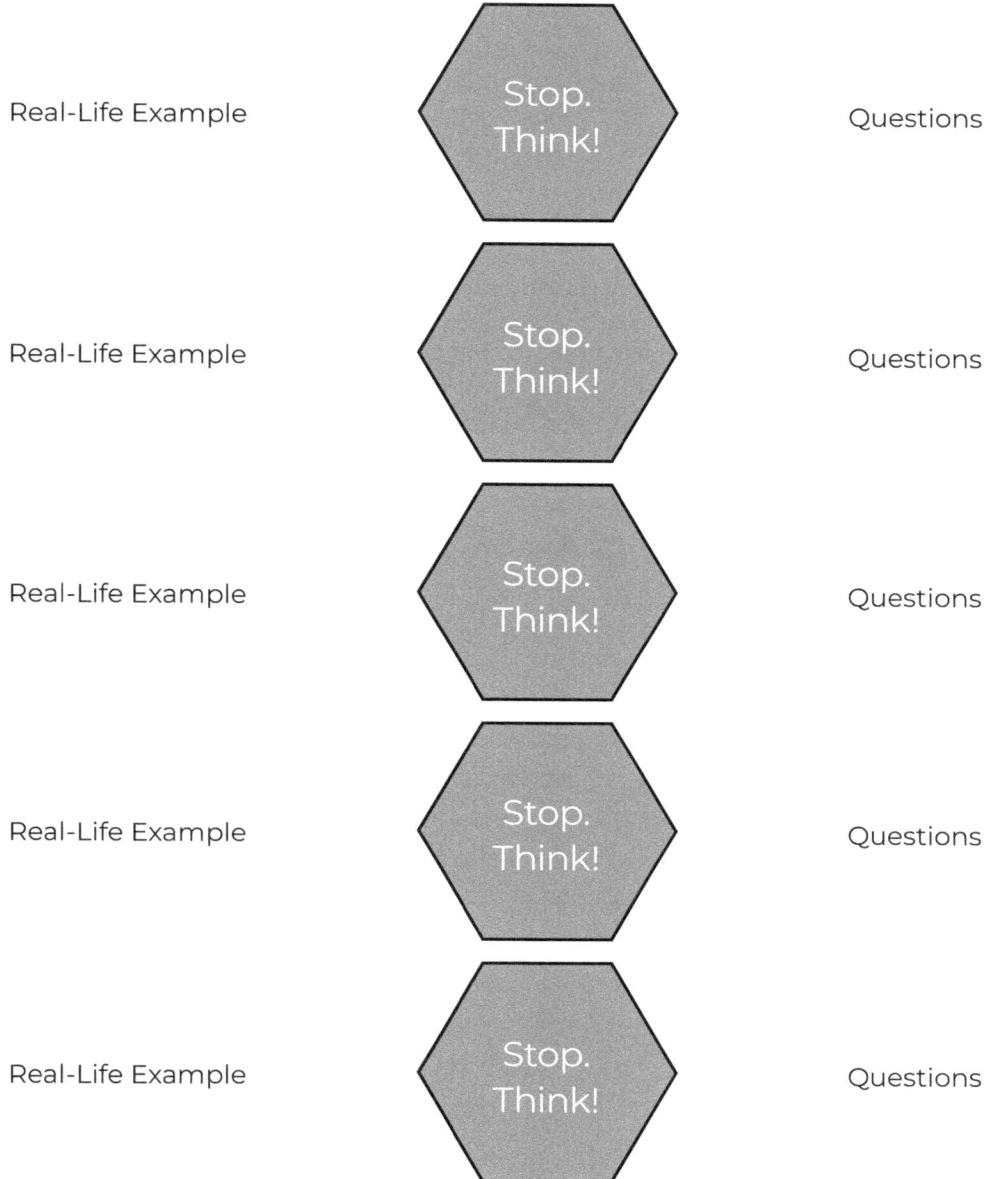

## 17. What Did You Say?

As you know, when you have ADHD, you may have some trouble with listening skills. With so many other things and so many distractions, your ADHD mind becomes fascinated with them. You might want to pay attention but find that you simply cannot. Sometimes instructions are very important, and they can make the difference between a good grade or a bad grade, or even provide you with safety measures for whatever action you are performing.

With this activity, you will listen to what your grownup says and then repeat the words back to them, exactly how they said it in the first place. Set a goal with your grownup. If you get that number of instructions or repetitions correct, then get a reward from your reward box.

## Here are a couple of examples to get you going.

1. Instruct your child about how to make their lunch for the next day.
2. Give your child instructions on how to organize a drawer or a box of items.
3. Tell your child a story about a cat and mouse.
4. Tell your child about a favorite part of a movie you like.
5. Explain to your child how to hard boil an egg.

## 18. Pick the Right Choice

Sometimes, it's hard to pick the right choice. Between all the exciting things that go on in the world, remembering all the rules gets tough! This activity will give you a chance to practice making the right choices so when it comes up in real life, you'll have an easier time remembering. Each column has a choice. Read them with your grownup and circle the one that you think is the right one.

| 1. You see something past the end of your yard, and you run out to see what it is. It's too shiny to pass up. | 1. You see something shiny past the end of your yard. You stop and think about what you should do. Instead of running to get the shiny thing, even though you want to, you turn around to ask your grownup if you can go. |
|---|---|

| | |
|---|---|
| 2. When you are doing homework, you start to become distracted. When you realize you're not paying attention to your homework anymore, you go downstairs and explain to your grownup that you need a break. You take a short break and then return and finish your homework by no longer being distracted. | 2. You start doing your homework and realize that your desk drawer needs to be organized and cleaned out. When you start cleaning it out, you find a lot of pencils in the drawer and notice that none of them are sharpened very much, and so you go to another room to get a sharpener. When you are there, you see something out of place in the kitchen, and you try to move it back into place. |
| 3. You are playing tag with your friend in your friend's backyard. When your friend tags you, you fall over and scrape your knee. Instantly, you get very angry and yell at your friend for pushing you over. You wind up calling your parents to come and get you because you no longer want to play with your friend. | 3. You and your friend are playing tag in their backyard. When your friend tags you, you fall over and scrape your knee. Although you get angry for a moment, you take a breath, close your eyes, and remember that you like your friend. You remind yourself that they wouldn't push you down on purpose. Once you work through your feelings, you get your scrape cleaned up and continue to play with your friend |

| 4. When you do homework on the computer, you know that there is the internet. On the internet, you find a video that everyone has been talking about at school. Then you start watching it. When that video is over, another one starts, and soon, you've watched ten videos. When your parent comes in to see how you are doing with your homework, you panic, turn the screen off, and try to come up with a story before they ask you what you are doing. | 4. When you do homework on the computer, you know that there is the internet. You and your parents come up with an idea about how you can do homework on the computer without being distracted by the internet. When you need a break, you can take one, and if you go on the internet during this time, you will go onto the internet on a different device. Going onto another device will help you get away from getting into the habit of being online when you are supposed to be doing homework. |
|---|---|

Now have your grownup write some choices down for you that are special to your house, your rules, and your environment.

|   |   |
|---|---|
|   |   |
|   |   |
|   |   |
|   |   |

## 19. Red Light, Green Light!

Red light, green light is a great game for listening skills, which is important to practice for children with ADHD. Plus, you can add it to any activity, such as putting away groceries, doing homework, putting shoes on, playing video games, and more! When you play "Red Light, Green Light!" a grownup will be the player calling the colors, and the child will listen to the instructions. The grownup can call "Red Light!" and the child has to stop what they are doing immediately. When the grownup calls "Green Light!" the child begins their task again. The point of this activity is for the child to learn instructions and to listen quickly with attention.

**If you are looking to play the game simply:**

1. Stand across the room or yard from one another.
2. The grownup faces the child and says, "Red light!" The child cannot move.
3. The grownup turns their back to the child and says, "Green light!" The child moves quickly to reach the grownup.
4. If the child tags the grownup before they turn back to face forward, the child wins!
5. If the child is moving when the grownup turns around, the child has to go back to the starting point and walk the distance all over again.

To work Red Light, Green Light! into your daily routine (for instance, when putting away the dishes from the dishwasher), the grownup can stand nearby and say "Red light!" for the child to wait to put the dishes away, and "Green light!" for the child to start putting them away again. Adding a timed experience to a chore can help the child get excited about doing something. Come up with a reward, like extra TV time or a favorite snack, to give your child when they complete the task by following all the "Red Light, Green Light!" instructions.

## 20. Bake a Cake

Nothing tastes better than baked goods made with your own hands. Now, it's time to bake your own cake. Be careful! You have to follow the instructions, or the cake won't turn out well.

With this activity, you can use a box of cake mix or make it from scratch. Below is a historical cake recipe. This cake is healthier because it doesn't have any frosting. If you would like to add a topping, try adding some fresh jam. It's also easy to make!

## Historical Cup Cake

*Supplies*

- Oven
- 8x8 cake pan
- 3 medium-sized bowls
- Measuring spoons
- Measuring cups
- 2 mixing spoons
- Whisk
- Cooking spray or parchment paper
- Aluminum Foil

## Ingredients

*Cake*

- 1 cup butter
- 2 cups sugar
- 3 cups flour
- 4 eggs

## Instructions

1. Preheat the oven to 350°.
2. Line your 8x8 baking pan with parchment paper, or spray the pan completely with cooking spray.
3. Mix all of the ingredients in a bowl.
4. Pour the cake batter into a pan.
5. Bake for 25 minutes or until golden brown.
6. Ask an adult to help test to see iff the cake if fully baked by sticking a toothpick or fork into the center. If not fully backed, return to the oven.
7. Cool cake for 20 minutes before eating.

## 21. Repeat the Beat!

This activity is a great one for listening skills. It takes two or more people to play, and you'll need something to beat your rhythm out on. Flip over bowls, pots, pans, plastic containers, or just beat out patterns and rhythms on the family table and get ready to play.

1. Using your hands, a spoon, or other stick, tap out one pattern onto the top of your "drum."
2. Start slowly so your child can keep up. First, just do one tap.
3. Your child will then repeat the tap.
4. Then you will do another rhythm, or you can just do two taps, like, tap, tap.
5. Your child should repeat your pattern.
6. Continue building on the "taps" until your child becomes challenged.
7. When they can't follow you on a tap, have them redo the same pattern, but first remind them of the pattern by tapping on your "drum."

8.  Make this activity timed. Only do it for 10 to 15 minutes to ensure that your child doesn't become distracted, overwhelmed, or frustrated.

9.  See what kind of beats you can come up with together!

## 22. Tell Me What You Are Doing

This activity incorporates self-coaching to help you stay on track and give you a chance to follow instructions to the T. When you tell yourself what you are doing and keep track of it, you will not miss any steps in your instructions at all.

If you are a grownup reading this, you can take the lead by showing your child what they need to do. Show by example. **If you are doing the laundry, you could say:**

"It's time to do the laundry."

"I'm taking the laundry basket to the laundry room."

"I am separating the clothes into colors."

"Black or dark clothes go here."

"Red, pink, and orange clothes go here."

"White clothes go there."

"I'm picking up a pile of clothes and putting them into the washing machine."

"I am adding the soap."

"I am turning on the washing machine."

"I will put the wet clothes in the dryer when they are done washing."

Having your child do the same thing when they do daily chores or hygiene habits (like brushing their teeth) will give them a straight line of directions to guide themselves into the next steps.

## 23. Simon Says

This game can be a fun and active way to burn energy or develop listening skills. It's important for children with ADHD to practice their listening skills. To make it more fun, add a reward to the end for however many instructions your child gets right, or flip it around where your child is giving the instructions, and you are following the orders. You can also do Simon Says with any chore around the house. This way, you are incorporating life skills into the mix, as well.

For a simple game of Simon Says, one person is "Simon," and the other player has to follow Simon's instructions. If the player fails to follow the instructions, they sit out for the round.

1. "Simon says, touch your head."
2. "Simon says, touch your knee."
3. "Touch your nose."
4. "Oops! I didn't say Simon Says."

When all players are out of the game, you can start a new round.

## 24. Questions & Answers

During any activity, but especially reading stories and during homework, asking questions to your child is a great way to keep them engaged in what they are doing. Having your child answer you back also lets you know that they are paying attention to what they are doing or what is going on. Make a habit of asking two to three questions during each 20-minute activity.

You don't have to ask questions about what has happened, and you can keep asking them questions about what they think will happen, as well. Adding anticipatory questions into the mix will help your child start to consider the consequences of their actions.

### For example, if you are reading Roald Dahl's novel Matilda, you can ask:

- "What do you think happens when the little boy steals a slice of cake?"
- "How do you think Matilda's parents will react when they find out?"
- "What did Matilda love to do the most before she went to school?"
- "Does Matilda have a magical power?"

**If you are asking them questions when they are doing homework, you can ask them questions like:**

- "What problem did you just solve? Can you explain it to me?"

- "What happened to this character in the story?"

Once you both get into the swing of this activity, it can become part of your healthy routine. Making a habit of this, you can build some really good cognitive skills that don't come easy for anyone with ADHD.

## 25. The Tower Game

The tower game gives your ADHD child a chance to stop, think, and then act instead of just reacting. You will need to use the board game Jenga or some similar three-dimensional block tower for this activity. **When the game is set up, you will need to do the following:**

1. Each player takes a turn one at a time.

2. The first player chooses one block from the tower and removes it from its place.

3. Then, the same player adds the block to the top of the building without knocking the building over.

4. The game continues in the same way for the rest of the players.

This game incorporates patience, thoughtfulness, and consequences.

Having your child wait their turn instills the idea of patience. Before your child takes their turn, they have to think about where the best place to take the block out will be. This is a three-tofive-second exercise in the examination. Then, they know the consequence of pulling the wrong block will be that the tower falls.

Remember, unless your child is wildly interested in this game, put a time limit on gameplay. This way, they don't become distracted, bored, or frustrated.

## 26. Would You Rather?

Playing the "Would You Rather" game with your child is a great way to give hypothetical options for real-life situations. Have them choose between two options, and when they pick one, ask them to explain why they chose the option they did. You can have some fun with this game by asking options that are a little weird or wacky, but make sure to incorporate plenty of life scenarios in the game. This game can be played almost everywhere, especially when you see your child's patience start to wane or their boredom spike up. **See a few examples below to get you started:**

1. Would you rather be an eagle or a walrus?

2. Would you rather have claws or paws?

3. Would you rather eat a cookie with ants on it or celery with peanut butter?

4. Would you rather make spaghetti with your toes or clean up your room?

# Healthy Body, Healthy Mind

*A comprehensive understanding of ADHD Health Support*

## Your Brain on Food

Everything you eat makes your body work. From how you write your name to the thoughts you think, each time you put something into your body, you are creating energy. That is why it is important to focus on what you are eating instead of just finding food that tastes good. Not all food that tastes good is good for you, and when you have ADHD, be extra careful because refined sugars and processed foods will affect your brain and body in a more obvious way.

Food has nutrients, chemicals, and other elements that energize the brain and ensure that it functions correctly. The odd thing about the brain is that even when the food isn't healthy for you, your brain can still react positively. This reaction happens because you enjoy the food you are eating, but just because your brain tells you that you enjoy what you are putting into your body doesn't make it healthy. Remember this when you are eating anything delicious, especially when the food is unhealthy.

Any time you eat a food you "love," chemicals arise in your brain. This action makes you feel happy. However, if you keep eating the food you "love," the chemical will start to go away. This reaction means that you have to eat more of the food to keep the happy feeling, and eating more unhealthy food means that you're putting more unhealthy stuff into your body.

So, to keep your body and brain working in a healthy way, you have to eat plenty of healthy, whole foods. The type of food you eat can affect your brain. When you eat healthy food, your brain will absorb healthy nutrients, which means your brain will react in a healthy way.

## The Positive and Negative Effects of Food

Scientists, doctors, and researchers have done a lot of tests and studies on the brain to see what food works best. Many of these studies show why healthy food is good for our brains and bodies, while unhealthy food has been found to harm your brain. See the list below for good food versus bad food to learn how they help or hurt activity in your mind.

Omega-3 Fatty Acids: Foods like fish and walnuts will help you feel happier, help you with learning, and give you a better memory as you get older.

Sugar: White, refined sugar is the worst for you. When you eat too much sugar, it affects many parts of your body, including your brain and your stomach. The more sugar you eat, the more your body becomes used to it. Eventually, you will start to develop a weakness for sugar. This reaction will lead to you not knowing when you are full, making it difficult to lose weight.

Fruits and Vegetables: This food group has a ton of healthy nutrients that will feed your brain and body in a great way. The chemicals and elements in fruits and vegetables can also help the cells in your body, which are like little taxis that drive good things around inside of you and help feed other organs. When you eat fruits and vegetables every day, your brain will help you stay more alert and help you with distractions.

Gluten: This food can be good or bad for you. However, many people are sensitive to gluten, and it is hard to test other than the fact that you feel better when you aren't eating it. If you have a gluten intolerance, your brain will become foggy, you'll feel sleepy, and you'll be grumpier more often.

## The Best Way to Eat

To make sure you pick the best foods for your body, ADHD, and brain, take note of what you are eating. This section will help teach you how to track your food, what foods are good and what foods are bad for your body, and how to make healthier choices, even if you really want to sneak something that is unhealthy for you. The better you treat your body on the inside, the better your body will treat you with your ADHD.

## 27. Coloring My Body with Healthy Food

The food you eat affects the way your body works. When you add unhealthy food, no matter how good it tastes, to your body, it starts to become sluggish and hard to do certain things. Then, your mind becomes slower, unfocused, and tired. Knowing what food to put into your body is a good thing. Color the images of the food and circle the healthy food that will help your body work the best way it can!

## 28. Brain Food

As you and your grownup have read, the better the foods you eat and the more exercise you do, the better your body will work overall. When your body works better, your ADHD works better, and the better things are working, the easier it is for you to do more stuff and find more ways to do something. Below is a list of words you should circle to understand better what type of exercise and food you should put into your body. When you are done circling the healthy items, make sure to color your brain and make it look nice!

I would like to add this doesn't mean you can never have a treat, rather to have treats every now and again and not something you consume every single day.

| | | |
|:---:|:---:|:---:|
| french fries | hot pockets | donuts |
| running | bananas | avocado |
| broccoli | watching tv | chocolate chip cookies |
| dancing | cake | carrots |
| salad | steak | chicken nuggets |
| walking | sleeping | baking |
| playing video games | basketball | talking on the phone |
| watching YouTube | going to a football game | pepperoni rolls |
| cupcakes | candy | frozen chicken nuggets |
| cooking | playing football | painting nails |
| reading | sitting outside | vegetable pizza |
| apples | strawberry | icecream |
| weight lifting | situps | pushups |
| potato chips | grilled cheese | tomatoes |
| cauliflower | eggs | blueberries |
| caramels | chicken | bacons |
| peppers | pop | water |
| fruit juice | energy bars | energy drinks |
| coffee | lunges | jumping jacks |
| jump rope | baseball | oatmeal |
| fish | mashed potatoes | skating |

## 29. What Can I Do?

Not only do you have to eat right, but you have to work your body and mind, too. Below is a list of examples that you can do to work your body and mind. Make a list with your grownup specific to you, your rules, and your lifestyle.

**EXAMPLE:** Listen to music for 15 minutes.

**EXAMPLE:** Paint a picture.

**EXAMPLE:** Go for a nature walk to look for new things in the woods.

_____
_____
_____
_____
_____
_____
_____
_____
_____
_____
_____
_____
_____
_____
_____
_____
_____
_____
_____

## 30. I'm Booooored. Now What?

There are going to be some days when things just get boring. When this happens, your ADHD can start to make you cranky, restless, depressed, or anxious. When you start feeling this way, you can read the list below and find something new you may want to try. These are indoor and outdoor activities, so whether you are having a rainy day or a sunny day, you'll be able to find something to keep you busy. Make sure to get adult permission first!

- Paint a picture
- Learn how to throw a curveball
- Play a board game
- Learn about hockey
- Find a new favorite funny YouTuber
- Learn how to roller skate
- Ride your bicycle
- Build a birdhouse
- Find the best way to wrap a present
- Find a new recipe to make for dinner
- Research how to knit a blanket
- Discover something new about cows
- Sew any holes that are in clothes
- Learn to draw an animal
- Listen to an audio book
- Make healthy cookies
- Figure out how to make a volcano
- Read a new book
- Play basketball
- Find a new way to walk around your block
- Write a poem
- Think about learning to ride a horse. Would you want to?
- Make dinner for your family
- Start knitting socks
- Research about a new part of the world
- Find the best way to do a sit-up
- Learn how to kick a soccer ball
- Start a puzzle
- Build a tall tower
- Learn about the planets
- Research more about how cars are made.
- Wash your bicycle
- Build a tent in your room with sheets and pillows
- See how many people there are in the world.
- Ask your parent to make a smoothie with you
- Watch a new movie
- Learn how to sew a stuffed animal
- Take a bath
- Find out how paper bags were made

- Tape a piece of paper to a window and trace an image from outside
- Add patches to pants
- Go bowling
- Play with your toys
- Color in a coloring book.
- Take a nap

## 31. Reading for Fun?

For someone with ADHD, reading may not be an idea of the best time. However, reading can nourish the mind in a great way. If you're not interested in sitting still and reading a book, try using an audiobook so you can hear the story. At the same time, you can do other things like organizing and cleaning your room, doing homework, exercising, or practicing a sport.

If you are looking for some audiobooks to start with, see some ideas below. You can add your ideas to the workbook, as well.

1. We are Water Protectors by Carole Lindstrom
2. The Giving Tree by Shel Silverstein
3. Winnie-The-Pooh by A. A. Milne
4. The Dog Man Series by Dav Pilkey
5. Love Hair by Matthew A. Cherry and Vashti Harrison
6. _____
7. _____
8. _____
9. _____
10. _____
11. _____
12. _____
13. _____
14. _____
15. _____
16. _____
17. _____
18. _____
19. _____
20. _____
21. _____

22. _____
23. _____
24. _____
25. _____
26. _____
27. _____
28. _____
29. _____
30. _____

## 32. Questions and Answers

Questions and answers can help your child stay in the moment as well as improve their memory. When you ask questions about healthy food and exercise, your child will begin to remember the information and start to incorporate healthy habits into their routines, even if they don't realize it's going on.

Here are a few questions you can ask your child about healthy food and good exercises. Feel free to add other questions below, too.

1. Is a candy bar healthy? Why or why not?
2. Why is exercise good for someone with ADHD?
3. How does eating healthy help out your brain?
4. If you are feeling nervous, what kind of exercise could you do to help?
5. What type of food is better for you, a red apple or red pepper?
6. _____
7. _____
8. _____
9. _____
10. _____
11. _____
12. _____
13. _____
14. _____
15. _____
16. _____
17. _____

18. _____
19. _____
20. _____
21. _____
22. _____
23. _____
24. _____
25. _____
26. _____
27. _____
28. _____
29. _____
30. _____

## 33. Guess the Good Food

Some foods can seem healthy when they really are not. While research means that our knowledge of foods is constantly growing and changing, knowing the basics and what to look for will help you and your child make the right food choice when there are too many options.

I would like to add this is not an exclusive guide to nutrition or dietary advice, it's mainly for kids to understand the basics of differentiating high sugar foods from wholesome foods etc.

This activity will have you and a grownup go through two choices each. One choice will be healthier than the other. Circle the one you think is going to be the most nutritious. Then, after you pick all the healthy choices, read the key below to find out if your answer is right.

| | |
|---|---|
| Low-Fat Flavored Yogurt | Greek Yogurt with Fresh Fruit |
| Microwave Popcorn | Whole Kernel Popcorn |
| Homemade chicken nuggets | Frozen chicken nuggets |
| Tortilla chips | Doritos |
| 2% Milk | Chocolate milk |
| Hot Cheese Dip | Cottage Cheese |
| Unsweetened Peanut butter | Fat-free Peanut butter |

| | |
|---|---|
| Onion rings | Pepper skewers |
| Roasted potatoes | French Fries |
| Fruit Smoothies | Smoothies Made with Fruit Juice |
| Sliced Apples | Flavored premade applesauce |
| Mini blueberry muffins | Granola breakfast bar |
| Pasta with semolina | Whole grain pasta |
| Banana and Almond Flour Pancakes | Pancakes from a box |
| Whole-Grain Cereal | Cereal with Enriched Wheat Flour |
| Egg salad made with low-fat mayo | Egg salad made with Avocado |
| Scrambled eggs made with Water and Cheese | Scrambled eggs made with olive oil and cheese |

**HEALTHY FOOD KEY:**

Greek Yogurt with Fresh Fruit, Whole Kernel Popcorn, Homemade chicken nuggets, Tortilla chips, 2% Milk, Unsweetened Peanut butter, Pepper skewers, Roasted potatoes, Fruit Smoothies, Slice Apples, Granola breakfast bar, Whole grain pasta, Whole-Grain Cereal, Egg salad made with Avocado, Scrambled eggs made with olive oil and cheese

## 34. Mindfulness & Meditation

Meditation and mindfulness are amazing for anyone. When you add it to your ADHD work, you begin to get comfortable with your thoughts and build some great tools for when stress levels have you knotted up.

The problem with meditation and mindfulness with someone who has ADHD is that it is sometimes hard to sit in one place for a long time. You should start by doing meditation for short periods first. You can follow the plan below and see how meditation works for you. Also, adding in some meditative music can help your mind begin to settle. However, the point of meditation is not to clear your mind of your thoughts; it is to learn to let your thoughts go after they come into your mind—even the hyper-focused ideas.

Mindfulness comes with meditation, but having a weekly practice where you and your grownup can see where you could have done something differently or had various choices to make can help spur the mindful process.

**Meditation Practice:**

*Day 1 through Day 7: Sit for 5 minutes with eyes closed.*

*Day 8 through Day 15: Sit for 7 minutes with eyes closed.*

*Day 16 through Day 23: Sit for 10 minutes with eyes closed.*

*Day 24 through Day 31: Sit for 12 minutes with eyes closed.*

Continue working up until you and your grownup hit 20 minutes. After that, sit for 20 minutes for a few months. If you need to play some meditative music while you do it, you should!

Remember, the point is not to get rid of your thoughts. The point of this meditation is just to listen to your thoughts and then let them go. Think of them as clouds that are floating through your mind, and you are watching them drift by.

If you find yourself getting fidgety, that's okay. Just reset yourself and continue trying for the allotted time—no need to start over. Meditation takes practice and patience, and no one can just fall into it. You'll slowly work up to being able to sit still for 5, 7, 10, and 12 minutes.

**Questions to Ask in Self-Reflection:**

1. How did the week go?

2. Did I get angry or throw a fit about anything? If so, how could I have reacted differently?

3. What was a time when I was more impatient than I could have been?

4. Was there a morning where I was running late? What did I do to run late? How can I do it differently so that I don't run late for that reason again?

5. Was there a day after school that I didn't get my homework done or had a hard time completing my homework? What was the reason? (Did I get distracted? Have a hard time with the homework? Was it too easy? Was it challenging?)

6. Was there a day that I got distracted easily and missed an important part of any instructions that led me to get hurt, get a lower grade, or miss out on a good opportunity?

7. How did my routine go each day?

8. What was the best part of the week?

9. What activities did I do that I didn't like?

10. What was the part of the week that could have gone better for me? How could I improve on it next time?

## 35. You Want me to do Yoga?

Studies show that yoga exercises not only encourage mindfulness and meditative thinking but also help to build physical strength. When you have ADHD, it may take a little more time and energy to learn how to focus, but yoga will be an amazing activity to do by yourself in short bursts of time—or with your grownup for a little longer bonding time.

**Some easy moves are below:**

| | |
|---|---|
| **Child's Pose** | |
| **Downward Facing Dog** | |

| | |
|---|---|
| **Warrior One** | |
| **Mountain Pose** | |
| **Tree Pose** | |

Cat Pose

## 36. Music & Me

Music is an incredible tool when looking to connect to any emotion. It also helps when you are trying to unwind and relax. There are thousands of instrumental, non-lyrical music pieces that will help calm an ADHD child in any moment it is needed. See a couple of suggestions below.

Roberts, Maddy Shaw. "10 Relaxing Pieces of Classical Music for Children." Classic FM, April 2020. https://www.classicfm.com/discover-music/relaxing-music-for-children/#:~:text=10%20relaxing%20pieces%20of%20classical%20music%20for%20children.

"12 Hours of Stunning Aquarium Relax Music." Youtube. Accessed November 18, 2021. https://www.youtube.com/watch?v=prfZFyp4XZk.

# ADHD at Home

*Getting into Regular Routines, Eating Healthy, Building Good Habits, and Playtime*

## 37. Pretend & Play

Giving your child an opportunity to play pretend will help them feel less isolated than children with ADHD tend to feel. When you are playing pretend, you are letting your imagination run wild and giving yourself a chance to live out new dreams, which may lead to an interest in something you may never have thought about.

Find a box, which can be Tupperware or a toybox, where you keep all types of dress-up clothes. Include costumes like doctor, prince/ss, or jungle explorer, and add in some toys that could be fun to play with, like stuffed animals, action figures, toy food, and more.

When it's time for this activity, there are a few things you can do to help the play along:

1. Keep it routine. Have the activity be at the same time, as much as possible, every day.

2. Time it. Children with ADHD can be engaged for a short time and then may lose focus or want to move to something else. Give them a timer or a time limit for play.

3. Rehearse possible life choices and outcomes with them. Ask them questions like "what happens if the jungle explorer loses their tools?"

4. Redirect if you see your child getting distracted, ask them to continue their

story for you, or request a new idea for play, "When your action figure was climbing the building, what was going to happen next?"

5. Once time is up, make sure that there is a clean-up period, as well.

Including this activity in a daily routine will help your child feel less isolated and help them practice sticking with a task. After a few months, you may find yourself redirecting them less and that their ability to focus more on one thing at a time has improved.

## 38. Helping at Home

Helping at home is a big part of ADHD. It will teach you to think about other people and learn about being organized. Organization is a key part of learning how to manage ADHD. Keeping your home, spaces, and areas picked up will give your mind a great way to relax.

Some things you can do to help out at home are:

1. Ask if your parents need help with anything every day.

2. Take on two daily chores like cleaning dishes or taking out the trash.

3. Clean up your stuff every day. Any time you are done with a task, pick up after yourself.

4. Clean your room at least once a week and keep your clothes, desk, and floor clear of stuff.

## 39. See It. Say It.

This activity works with object permanence. Object permanence is where the "out of sight, out of mind" adage comes from. When a child with ADHD doesn't see something, it can be completely forgotten about. This exercise will help them remember that just because something isn't in their line of sight doesn't mean it is gone for good. When a child sees something throughout the day, encourage them to say the words. Examples can be:

- "I see the pencil."
- "I am putting the pencil into the desk."
- "The pencil is now in my desk."

When they say things out loud, they will begin to form a habit of reminding themselves where things are.

## 40. Memory

Memory is a card matching game that allows your child to work on memory skills. Like the activity above, the game Memory will help your child with object permanence and give them an opportunity to know that items are still present, even when they cannot see them.

You can play memory with a standard card deck or buy specialized memory matching cards. If you're looking to do something a little different, get twelve to twenty plastic cups and add small tokens or trinkets under them.

## 41. Have Fun with It!

Chores can be really boring, especially if you have ADHD. The sameness of an activity is one thing that really causes the ADHD mind to swerve in a different direction. The best thing to do is to have fun with the chores.

Some examples of having fun with ADHD will be:

1. Use a timer and race to see how quickly you can get something done, like clean a room, wash the dishes, or fold clothes. Try to be the time before and keep track. Make sure to have a reward system for when they beat their previous time.

2. Although racing against themselves can be fun, change up the activity so your ADHD child can keep up some spontaneous action. Race against them in doing a chore, like raking leaves, putting dishes away, or cleaning a room.

3. If you're looking for a different way to put things away, have your child put their socks, shirts, or items in a desk drawer in some kind of pattern. Then

have your child explain the pattern to you.

How else can you have fun with chores? Come up with a few new ideas specific to your home, lifestyle, and rules.

## 42. Find an Item, Put It Away!

Finding items in the house is a great way to incorporate mystery and amusement into tasks that may seem boring to anyone with ADHD. Have your grownup name certain things in the home or your bedroom. Have them time you, and then as soon as you see the item, you have to put it away in the right way.

This exercise will help you see how keeping things clean can help you find things quicker and easier.

## 43. Decorate Your Workspace

Having an engaging and colorful workspace can help anyone with ADHD get excited about doing their work. Get a corkboard, dry erase board, or calendar that you can write reminders on so you can always see what is coming up.

Also, having pencils, tools, notebooks, and other items that are your favorite colors or have your favorite characters on them will stimulate your home learning activities.

## 44. Sing-a-Long

Children learn really well with singing and songs. When you or your child are doing something less than fun or are becoming distracted by other things, start singing and encourage them to sing along. Your child will get into a habit of singing, which can help them in every corner of their life.

## 45. How About a Board Game?

Board games are amazing ways to learn about rules, how to take turns, and the consequences of your choices. Below is a quick list of a few games that help enhance your child's intelligence while working around some ADHD parameters. Remember, though, start with a short amount of time. Don't overwhelm your child with a new game. Give them a chance to find games that they enjoy.

**Chess:** According to the ADHD Treatment with Chess website, the practice of chess can influence your child's intellectual development. There are many instances where chess helps with emotional intelligence and contributes to the development of cognitive abilities.[13]

**Chutes & Ladders:** This game will help children with ADHD build tolerance for frustrating situations. When they see their game piece slide down the chute, they will begin to become frustrated, but soon they will see how quickly and easily the game turns around with just a little patience.

**Sudoku:** When a child feels bored, this game is a great way to fill up their time, keeping their hands busy and their minds challenged. While they need to know their numbers from 1 through 9 for this game, Sudoku can be very helpful when there is a little bit of pent-up energy.

**Chinese Checkers:** This game will help children learn how to anticipate consequences. If they set their marble in one space, chances are, another player will swoop down and create a complication for your child's color marbles. This exercise is a good one for them to look at their options and see what could happen instead of stomping their feet in frustration.

**Tic, Tac, Toe:** This game gives your child great practice in decision-making. If they choose the wrong box, they can lose the game or lose out on an opportunity. Plus, creating a tic, tac, toe board is easy, cost-efficient, and can be replicated in many places.

---

13. "ADHD Treatment with Chess - Educational Chess Tools." ADHD & Chess.

# ADHD at School

*Getting into Being in Class, Lunch & Recess, Building Good Habits with Homework*

The idea of having a routine may make your ADHD child balk, but once they get into a good groove, they will see how beneficial having a schedule is for them. Their brain will work more clearly, their work will be more concise, and other executive function skills will develop cleanly. While some readers of this book may not be in school yet, eventually, they will be. Having habitual, everyday activities that happen at the same time will help prepare your child for when they have to add new things to their daily lives.

## 46. First Thing in the Morning

No one can predict everything that is going to happen on any given occasion. However, having a list of what happens during their morning routine can help your child with the daily anticipation of what is expected and guide them on what their next task should be. They don't have to carry their list with them in a notebook or cross anything off to feel accomplishment, but having them review the list each day after school can give them an idea of what they missed or where they could improve upon.

**For an example list, see below:**

1. Wake up
2. Before doing anything, check your daily planner or calendar to see what your day is going to look like

3. Get dressed, put dirty clothes with dirty laundry

4. Eat breakfast, place dirty dishes in the sink

5. Brush teeth, put toothpaste and toothbrush away

6. Brush hair put the brush away

7. Get shoes on

8. Grab lunch box and book bag

9. Head out to bus/car to get to school.

10. At school, take out all homework from bookbag for the day

11. Place lunchbox and backpack in the assigned place

12. Put all papers in assigned boxes/hand in homework

13. Take out pencil and paper to get started

## 47. Lunch & Recess

Lunch and recess are great for socializing, resetting brains, and burning some excess energy. However, there are also going to be a lot of distractions. Lunchroom decisions can induce impulse control and extra hyperactivity. Talk to your child often about the right and wrong choices of nutrition and talk with their teachers about having a wind-down time so they can transition from recess back into classroom behavior again.

You can have a plan put in place for your child, perhaps have a discussion with the administration and see what is possible. Teachers have many students to look after, so having certain tools available may not be accessible. Still, if your child already has an Individual Education Plan (IEP) or 504-Plan in place, you and the group advocating for your child should be able to add certain measures to the program.

An example could be that if your child misbehaves in class, they do not skip recess because that will only help build up extra energy. However, they will still need to have some form of consequence, which could be up to you and your teachers to decide. Instead, it is important to find a consequence that aligns directly as a result of the child's actions (Example: If a child is not being safe with scissors, then the child would have the consequence that they are only allowed to use scissors under adult supervision.)

## 48. Coming Home

While it may seem daunting to schedule much of your child's day, when you have ADHD, it is a necessary part of helping them function. Plus, once they get into a good routine, the feeling of being scheduled to the nth degree will transition into a streamlined part of the day. There will always be blips and bruises on any given occasion, but keeping a schedule as best as possible will help create a sense of calm in what could end up being chaos.

**TO KIDS:** When you and your grownup sit down to talk about your routine as you come home, think about the following:

1. Where should you keep your planner or list of homework you need to do?

2. Do you need time to let your brain rest from school, or do you want to get your homework over with?

3. Do you have a place to put your book bag, shoes, and paperwork that needs to be seen by grownups?

4. Do you want to eat a snack when you come home? Can you put healthy snacks in a special "afterschool" bin/drawer/basket so you can easily grab them and they are in your line of sight?

5. Do you change your clothing into something more comfortable?

6. If you need a break, can you set a timer on when it's the right time to start doing homework? What are the rules for your break? How long do you have? What can you do? Where can you go? These are all questions that you can talk about to make your transition home better.

7. If you need some time to wind down, is it best if you take a meditative break, lie down, and listen to calming music? Or do you need to burn that extra energy?

8. When do you get to play with friends?

9. When do chores need to be completed?

Having a plan in action is a great way for you all to know what is expected of your child and the rules for afterschool time.

If your child cannot read well yet, make a list of icons and images that show their tasks. When they complete each task, have them put a sticker by the image or cross something off. Allowing your child to interact with their schedule can give them the motivation to complete more.

## 49. Chair or No Chair

It's a well-known fact that it can be hard for you to sit still with ADHD. There are times when even sitting in a chair with a fidget spinner can still have you squirming. So, sit down with the grownups and teachers to see what you can do about standing in class if you need to.

If you are standing in class, you should still be at your desk, and you cannot disturb other children. Still, standing may give you an option to feel less fidgety and help you be more focused on the tasks your teacher is asking you to complete.

## 50. Desk Cleanliness

If you are looking to build a routine at school, it's important to know what expectations your teacher has for your cleanliness and organization. You should take time each week to clean out your desk and organize your tools, books, papers, and more.

Suppose it helps you to have containers or baskets where each item should be. In this case, talk with your parents and teacher to see if they can get you some. Make sure the containers are fun colors and have your favorite shapes or characters on them, so you keep wanting to use them!

Also, make sure the top of your desk is cleared away of any clutter. That will help you stay more focused when you need to pay attention to the teacher.

If you have a chance each day to clean out your desk, then you should take that time and do it. Keeping your desk clean and organized will give you a great opportunity to help your brain work the best way it possibly can.

## 51. Fun Pens, Pencils, Notebooks, and More!

While keeping organized is important, helping your child stay engaged in class can help, too. Having decorative pencils and other writing implements will give them a chance to be excited to use them. This also includes notebooks with fun designs and maybe some stickers, which you can give them as good feedback. Any little thing helps!

## 52. Positive Feedback, Positive Results

As someone with ADHD, you do REALLY well when you get positive feedback on how you are doing with tasks, projects, homework, and more. Try to get your teacher or IEP aid to provide you with feedback on your work. Feedback means that they will tell you all the places you've done something right at, and they will help you find the areas where you can improve. When you get positive feedback about what you are doing, you'll find that you want to do more work and look for future ways to feel that pride in yourself.

## 53. Fidget Tools, Anyone?

While fidget spinners were all the rage throughout elementary, middle, and high schools a few years ago (and have been banned in many places because they distracted as opposed to soothing students who didn't have ADHD), fidget tools are a great use for you when you have ADHD. If you can talk with your teacher and grownups about how to use these tools in your daily school life, it may be able to give you a little break when you find your mind wandering. These tools can also allow you to refocus back on your work and keep doing well throughout the day.

# Friends & Family

*How to Treat Other People How YOU Want to Be Treated*

## 54. Time to Take Turns

Teaching children with ADHD to take turns is an important part of their ADHD management. Taking turns can be especially difficult because it includes two things that the ADHD mind doesn't want to do: be patient and avoid instant gratification.

So, what you can do is practice taking turns. Even when you are at home, have your child wait to do anything they are looking forward to doing. Include standing in line and offer games they can play to keep them distracted while they wait in line. The game "I SPY" is a great way to keep the ADHD mind occupied as your child guesses what you are looking at. You can also make up "waiting" songs or develop other games that are specific to your home, lifestyle, and house rules.

Having your child wait in line for meals, bathrooms, games, playing, or anything they will enjoy in everyday life will help them prepare for when they have to wait in line, take turns, or delay gratification in unique experiences.

## 55. Practice Kindness with Words

If there is one thing a child with ADHD is not afraid of, it is speaking their mind. Often, harsh or critical words are said to other people when your child makes their opinion clear. However, they work best with positive feedback, so have them use kind words with others.

## For this activity:

1. Find and decorate a jar or basket.

2. Write out a list of ten to twenty positive ways to describe someone or something, even if those words are critiques.

3. Cut these words from the paper in strips or squares.

4. Fold the squares of paper up and put them in the jar or basket.

5. Each day pick a new word for your child to learn and use all day.

6. They will use this for other people and themselves.

Doing this activity will have your child learn new words and how to use them, along with giving your child an idea of how to give constructive feedback when they are in social settings.

## Some words to use, for example, are:

| improve | mistake | learning |
| :---: | :---: | :---: |
| goals | kind | pretty |
| review | opinions | develop |
| facts | describe | support |

## 56. Share & Share Alike

Now it's time to learn about sharing. Sharing can go hand-in-hand with taking turns, learning about patience, and delaying impulses. When you start a sharing activity, understand that your child may become anxious and frustrated, but these feelings should lessen the more you continue to work with sharing.

## What You Need:

1. Two boxes—these can be decorated.

2. A bunch of interesting objects.

3. A friend or family member to share things with.

## Instructions:

1. Set a timer for 10 minutes to start—work your way up to 30. Gauge your child's demeanor, and you can move the time up or down depending on their mood of the day.

2. Hand your child a toy or object from one box, and ask them to hand you a toy or object from the other.

3. Each of you plays with the object for about 3 to 5 minutes. See how your child reacts to seeing you or a family member have fun with something they can't have at first.

4. If they wait patiently for their turn, you can hand it to them to play with at the end of your time, as long as they pass another object for you.

5. Continue this practice as long as your child's mood stays even and until the time you set is up.

6. It's best to do this type of game daily so your child becomes accustomed to sharing. However, it may not always be practical, so try to do this activity at least three times a week.

## 57. Helping Hand at Home

Helping out at home is something that every person living in the house should do. When you help your grownups around the house, you show that you appreciate how much they help you out. There are age-appropriate tasks and chores that you can do to help out around the house, too.

Each day, you should offer to help out with at least one thing besides your daily chores. To come up with how to help, make a "helping wheel" with your grownups, or draw ideas from a fun basket you design specifically for this purpose.

Each time you offer to help someone, you show that you are thinking about others, being kind, and treating others how you want to be treated.

### What are some chores you can help with?

- Sweeping
- Cleaning your room
- Picking up your toys

- Feeding a pet

- Doing the dishes

- _____

- _____

- _____

- _____

## 58. Helping Hand at School

School can sometimes be a little boring, and you might get a little too fidgety. Have a plan set up between you, your grownups, and your teacher so that when you begin to get jittery, you can start helping out in the classroom.

Each day, you can ask the teacher if they need help. You should not offer to help when you are taking a test or anytime your classmates need to concentrate. **Some examples of how you can help at school are:**

1. Pass out paperwork

2. Clean off boards

3. Pick up toys/games/objects after group play

## 59. Writing Letters to Friends

Some days you might have a bad day. When you are, you also might get snappy with friends and family. Behaving this way can often hurt other people's feelings, and there are times, with ADHD, you might not be thinking about that. However, thinking about how your actions affect other people is extremely important, especially if you treat your friends with kindness and respect.

If you think that you have hurt someone with words and actions, or if your friends tell you that you've hurt them with your comments or actions, don't let your embarrassment pump up your emotions. Instead, listen to what they said, take a breath, and wait to respond. When you come home, write a letter to them, add everything they said that hurt your feelings in their letter, and see how you would want to be treated at that moment.

Thinking about something from another person's perspective will let you start to see many things in many ways. When you write things down, you'll be able to see them clearly, and it should help you bring the ideas into a little more focus.

## 60. Structured Play with Friends

The biggest thing when dealing with friends is getting together and having fun. Talk to your parents about having a friend come over at least once a week for a couple of hours so you can get to know them and have fun together. When you are playing with friends, you'll have to learn how to share and treat them with kindness and respect. You'll have to treat them how you would want to be treated. But remember, keep it to a certain amount of time, and have your grownups plan out some activities beforehand so you can stay entertained while they are there.

### Some ideas for playing with friends are:

| Dress Up and Pretend | Board Games | Playing at the Park |
| Dance Party | Riding Bikes | Scavenger Hunt |
| Baking Together | Dinner with Friends | Video Games and Snacks |

# Getting Ready

Learn How to Prepare for Each Day, Even When it Seems Too Hard

### 61. Prep List for Tomorrow

Each day may not be the same, but you can have a specific routine to build something easy for you. Writing a list for tomorrow will help you get ready for each day and give you a chance to know already what you have to do. Writing things down will encourage the visualization that you need to help your brain remember them.

Make a list with your grownup, and make sure you have everything on the list you will need to do. **An example list can look like this:**

- Wake up
- Get dressed
- Make bed
- Put dirty clothes in hamper
- Put on shoes
- Eat breakfast
- Get jacket and backpack on
- Go to school
- Eat lunch
- Come home from school
- Eat snack
- Do homework
- Do chores
- Relax, TV time, game time
- Eat dinner, help clean up
- Get ready for bed

### 62. Good Days. Bad Days.

Everyone, even those who do not have ADHD, has bad days. Everyone also has good days. The difference we all make when we have bad days is by giving each other support and finding a way to shake out the badness.

However, activities for shifting gears from having a bad day can be pretty difficult. When your mindset is in a rough headspace, you may not want to do anything but take a nap. If that is the case, then do it! The point of having bad days is figuring out what you need to help yourself feel better and comfortable. See below for a few more ideas, but coming up with some activities that fit the rules of your house, the lifestyle you have, and your family members is a good way to practice getting out of negativity. Make a list of these ideas so you have something to turn to when you are feeling low. Trying to come up with something at the moment tends to be a bit too difficult.

## Examples of how to help yourself include:

| Go for a walk | Ride your bike | Journal |
| Take a nap | Curl up on the couch | Watch a movie |
| Drink hot tea | Paint, draw, make crafts | Clean up somewhere |

## 63. Clothing, Pajamas, Drawers, & Closets

Clothing can be a particularly difficult thing to maintain. But if it isn't put away nicely, you'll definitely notice. Making sure that your closets and drawers are organized is an amazing way to help yourself get ready for each day. Keep your socks with your socks, your shirts with your shirts, and each shoe with the matching shoe.

You might have to clean this up once a week until you get into the habit of keeping things organized, but after you get in the habit, you shouldn't have a hard time finding anything around your room.

## For an idea, try something like this:

| Fold up matching socks and keep them together | Put all underwear in the same drawer |
| Fold all t-shirts and put them in one drawer | Add all PJs to the same drawer |
| Keep your long-sleeve t-shirts together | Put sweatpants in one drawer |

| | |
|---|---|
| Keep sweaters/sweatshirts together in closet | Put any "fanicer" clothes into your closet. Hang dresses, skirts, and button-down shirts up. |
| Match all shoes together. Keep them lined up in your closet. | Organize your closet by type of clothing. Keep polo shirts and long-sleeve button shirts together. Keep all pants together. |
| Put athletic shoes in one place. | Keep athletic clothes together. |

## 64. Shoes & School Tools

Some kids have school shoes and play shoes. In other homes, it may not matter. Shoes are easily left out in different places around the house because when your child wants to get comfortable, shoes are the first thing to go. Plus, you may have a rule that they take their shoes off when they come home to avoid getting dirt or mud in the rest of the house.

Keeping shoes and school supplies near one another and in a designated space every day is a good practice for everyone to get into. If the whole family participates in this activity, the mornings can be less disorganized, and everyone can get out of the house quickly.

Keeping your jackets, shoes, and winter accessories in the same place can also give you a sense of organization. Your ADHD child will always know where to find gloves, hats, coats, book bags, and shoes if they are together.

This organization means that there is also less frustration and more ease for the entire house.

## 65. Rooms & Work Areas

Getting bedrooms and workspaces cleaned and organized so that your ADHD child has a system that works best for their brain will take a little time. But having these areas cleared away, especially the areas where your child spends most of their time, will help them focus more and allow them to steer clear of distractions.

Buying or making tools that can help your child organize will be a big incentive. Having decorative baskets, boxes, pencils, pens, and more can engage your child when they may otherwise feel like they just want to forget about homework and do other things.

# I Am Ready!

*A Daily Checklist for Students to Ensure They are Prepped for a Full Day*

### 66. A Gold Star for Good Behavior

Now that you are on the right road toward your best functioning self, you'll be getting more rewards and more gold stars! Remember to keep your rewards box full, but also get some other kind of rewards going. A sticker book or a chart where you get stickers for each day that you reach every goal is a great way to monitor yourself. This chart would be yours and yours alone, where you would go through your daily list and check off the items you have done for the day.

If you are interested in giving yourself a reward or having your parents give you a reward, it will be great if you research some bigger things and make a plan for what rewards you can get for two weeks, four weeks, six weeks, and three-month marks. You can keep going with rewards after that, too, but talking to a grownup about this will give you a chance to make sure you come up with the best plan possible.

### 67. Build Your Own Checklist

When you create a daily checklist, make sure the tasks on the list are important, needed, and key for each day. Have grownups help you come up with a list of tasks that don't need to be done each day but should be done on a weekly basis. Along with school, chores, and play, you build your checklist to your liking. Even if there are some tasks on the list you really don't want to do, know that these projects are important and will help you maintain your ADHD to its fullest potential.

## A sample checklist can look like this:

- Wake up on time
- Put dirty PJs in hamper
- Put school supplies in order
- Play at recess with friends
- Come home
- Do homework
- Leftover chores
- have downtime

- Brush Teeth
- Put dishes in sink
- Turn in all homework
- Put all homework and paperwork in "home" folder
- Put all school stuff away
- Eat dinner
- Brush teeth
- pick clothes out for tomorrow

- Eat a healthy breakfast
- Get to bus on time
- Eat healthy lunch
- Double-check bookbag to make sure I have everything I need.
- Eat healthy snack
- help grownups clean up
- read a book
- Go to bed by 9:00 p.m.

## 68. Reflecting on You

Journaling can keep your mind at ease, and it can help you see things that you may not be able to see otherwise. It's important to take time out for yourself and check in with your feelings, too. There will be times when you don't understand where your mistakes are or the feelings you're having about an issue.

Doing some self-reflection about instances that may have bothered you will help you understand where you can make improvements and will guide you into being the best version of yourself you can be.

## 69. What Else Are You Missing?

When you have an ADHD brain, you will most likely forget things. A lot. Each time you are getting ready to leave the house, school, or another place, stop and ask, "What am I missing?"

This question will take some time to get used to, and there still may be days when you might forget something; everyone does, it's totally normal!But if you can lower the number of days that you forget one thing, you are making good progress.

The point of this exercise is to help you become more aware of what you're doing at the moment, and it will give you some future planning skills that are hard for anyone with ADHD to think about.

## 70. You're Ready!

Every day, your child can implement at least one activity in this book. Together, you will have good and bad days even with a system in place. These moments should be looked on as learning moments and not seen as a means for punishment.

Anyone with ADHD works better with positive feedback and reinforcement. Getting into a routine will help build your patience with your child and give you both an opportunity to grow.

The routines will only be the start of ADHD management and should be taken in baby steps. Consistency is vital to help produce the best results for your child and give them the best upbringing you can provide them.

There will be chances for excitement and times of frustration, but as long as you keep growing, showing, and caring, your child will see how lucky they are and will appreciate everything you've done for them.

# References

"Celebrity Spotlight: How Michael Phelps' ADHD Helped Him Make Olympic History." Understood.org, October 2020. https://www.understood.org/articles/en/celebrity-spotlight-how-michael-phelps-adhd-helped-him-make-olympic-history.

"Celebrity Spotlight: Why Journalist Lisa Ling Was 'Relieved' by Her ADHD Diagnosis." Understood.org, October 2020. http://www.understood.org/articles/en/celebrity-spotlight-why-journalist-lisa-ling-was-relieved-by-her-adhd-diagnosis.

"Is ADHD a Learning Disability?" Medical News Today. Accessed November 18, 2021. https://www.medicalnewstoday.com/articles/is-adhd-a-learning-disability.

Morin, Amanda. "8 Common Myths About ADHD." Understood.org, February 2021. https://www.understood.org/articles/en/common-myths-about-adhd.

"Research on ADHD." Centers for Disease Control and Prevention, April 2019. https://www.cdc.gov/ncbddd/adhd/research.html.

"Understanding Executive Functioning Issues in Your Child." Understood.org, October 2020. https://www.understood.org/articles/en/understanding-executive-functioning-issues-in-your-child.

"Video: Activist David Flink on Growing up with ADHD and Dyslexia." Understood.org, October 2020. https://www.understood.org/articles/en/video-activist-david-flink-on-growing-up-with-adhd-and-dyslexia.

"What is ADHD?" Centers for Disease Control and Prevention, September 2021. https://www.cdc.gov/ncbddd/adhd/facts.html.

# Resources for Grown-ups

Zyppia. "21 Activities for Children with ADHD." Its Psychology, September 2021. https://itspsychology.com/activities-for-children-with-adhd/.

"ADHD Treatment with Chess - Educational Chess Tools." ADHD & Chess, January 2020. https://adhd-chess.com/#:~:text=Chess%20has%20become%20a%20powerful%20educational%20tool%20because.

Editors, ADDitude. "Play Therapy Techniques and Games to Try at Home." ADDitude, May 2021. https://www.additudemag.com/fun-games-help-adhd-children-learn-from-play/.

# Resources for Kids

"12 Hours of Stunning Aquarium Relax Music." Youtube. Accessed November 18, 2021. https://www.youtube.com/watch?v=prfZFyp4XZk.

"15 Fun and Easy Yoga Poses for Kids." Body Hiit Workout, October 2021. https://bodyhiitworkout.com/yoga-poses-for-kids/.

Cole, Lauran. "The Best Games for ADHD Kids: Mentalup." MentalUP, August 2020. https://www.mentalup.co/blog/attention-games-for-adhd#:~:text=ADHD%20Games%20and%20Activities%201%202-%20Red%20Light.

Giselle. "58 Fun and Easy Yoga Poses for Kids (Printable Posters)." Kids Yoga Stories, October 2020. https://www.kidsyogastories.com/kids-yoga-poses/.

"How the Food You Eat Affects Your Brain." Youtube. Accessed November 18, 2021. https://www.youtube.com/watch?v=xyQY8a-ng6g.

Roberts, Maddy Shaw. "10 Relaxing Pieces of Classical Music for Children." Classic FM, April 2020. https://www.classicfm.com/discover-music/relaxing-music-for-children/#:~:text=10%20relaxing%20pieces%20of%20classical%20music%20for%20children.

www.ingramcontent.com/pod-product-compliance
Lightning Source LLC
Chambersburg PA
CBHW080324080526
44585CB00021B/2457